Battling the Enemy Within

Exposing Satan's Ally Living Inside of Us All

By

LARRY SHELBY, JR.

LARRY SHELBY, JR.

Battling the Enemy Within

Destiny House Publishing, LLC

P.O. Box 19774 Detroit, MI   48219

Destiny House Publishing, LLC

www.destinyhousepublishing.com

inquiry@destinyhousepublshing.com

All scriptures are from King James Version unless otherwise stated.

ISBN: 978-1-936867-37-0

DEDICATION

This book is dedicated to my dad, Apostle Larry Shelby Sr., who, for as long as I have known him, has lived a Godly life, not only before the congregation, but at home, in front of his whole family. He has been an example to me as a man, a father, a husband, and a minister. Thank you for not only being my natural father, but also my father in the Gospel.

This book is also dedicated to my beautiful wife, Sherell Shelby, who has walked this life's journey with me for the past 25 years. I do not fully have the words to express my gratitude for your endurance, while I was trying to figure this all out. Thank you for never letting me quit, seeing through my excuses, and for not taking no for an answer. Thank you for being my biggest fan. I love you.

CONTENTS

BATTLING THE ENEMY WITHIN

ACKNOWLEDGMENTS

"Now thanks be to God who always leads us in triumph in Christ, and through us diffuses the fragrance of His knowledge in every place." (II Corinthians 2:14 NKJV)

Much gratitude to my coach and editor, Prophetess Crystal Jones, at Destiny House Publishing, Inc., for kicking me in the tail every chance she got. Without whose help, I'd still be writing this book.

To my pastor, Apostle Dr. Angela L. Thibeaux, thank you for supporting and walking with me over the years, as I journeyed through and unpacked the burdens of my soul.

To my parents, Apostle Larry Shelby Sr. and First Lady Lena Shelby, thank you for just being my parents and loving me. And, thank you for laying my foundation, and for stirring in me a love for our Heavenly Father.

To Apostle Eva Powel Grant, I have much gratitude for you standing with my wife and I in prayer, through all of our transitions. Your prayers covered us.

To my friend and brother in the Gospel, Apostle Kelvin

Easter, who's mentoring and coaching through Leading Edge Legacy Inc., helped to reignite my passion for leadership, at a pivotal time in my life.

To Apostle Kenneth Rhymes and Prophetess Jacquelyn Rhymes, thank you for being my surrogate parents, at a time in my life when I needed you most. Your deposit of honor and love will never be forgotten.

To my big brother in Christ, Pastor Robert Fifer, you have truly been like my blood brother. And it has been the greatest joy to serve alongside of you in ministry.

And, last, but certainly not least, to my best friend, Robert "Bob" Barber, to whom I've been able to talk about any and everything. You said that I spoke into your life as you birthed your YouTube channel. You have definitely returned the favor and spoken into my life to help bring this book to fruition. Thank you.

Thank you all.

"[I] give thanks to God always for you all, making mention of you in [my] prayers, remembering without ceasing your work of faith, labor of love, and patience of hope in our Lord Jesus

Christ in the sight of our God and Father, knowing, beloved

brothers [and sisters], your election by God."

Introduction

In your walk of faith, you may have fallen so many times that there seems to be no hope of ever changing. Sin seems to gain the advantage over you in certain areas of your life, despite your love for God. Proverbs 24:16 says, "A righteous man may fall seven ties and rise again..." (NKJV) That's seven times in one day. Christ, in Matthew 18:22, speaks with his disciples about the Godly response of forgiving your brother seventy times seven in a day. So the question is, if he falls that much, then what makes him righteous? The Apostle Paul says in Romans 7:21 "When I desire to do what is right, with me the evil is present." (YLT) So, if that was Paul's experience, then how did he go on to become one of the most prolific writers of The New Testament? The answers to these questions and more are shared on these pages. These chapters will help you initiate biblical disciplines, erase debility thought patterns, and develop new strategies to combat your most powerful enemy, yourself.

However, tactics alone are not enough to bring you deep spiritual, and lasting victory. Any motivational speaker or self-help guru can show you innovative strategies, new practices, and how to "think outside of the box". This book, however, will help you discover the "who" behind the "what". These pages will reveal the person behind the practices. That person is Christ. Learn how your relationship with Him, and your obedience to His word, will allow you to walk in true freedom. His freedom will give you real power and complete victory in this life, and your life to come.

Chapter 1
Know Your Enemy

He Definitely Knows You

No matter what the newspapers, news networks, or social media have to say, there is a world war going on every day, on every continent, and in every country on the face of the earth. Like any other war we've ever known, there are casualties, prisoners, and victors. Unfortunately, most people don't know that they are even in a war. This war is silent. It is covert. And it is also spiritual. Those of us that are unaware, sometimes fail to:

1) understand how important it is to win this war,

2) understand to what extent our enemy is willing to go to win, and

3) realize even who our enemy really is.

The average believer is oblivious to what he or she is up against. As a result, we are often blind-sided by our enemy's entire mode and style of warfare. We must understand that this is not a "fair" fight. Our enemy doesn't fight according to man-made rules of fairness, nor does he fight with honor. As a matter of fact, he often has assistance from an uncanny ally. We fight these battles on more than one front, because we have more than one enemy. Most believers understand Satan to be our great enemy, however, he's not our only enemy. We concentrate so much on Satan that we fail to even think of any other adversary, especially one that is even closer to us, and even more dangerous than Satan himself. Our enemy is us. To be more precise, it is our flesh.

The Strong's Concordance of the Bible defines the word flesh as: (G4561) sarx

Definition: 1. flesh (as stripped of the skin) that is (strictly) the meat of an animal (as food) or 2. (By extension) the body (as opposed to the soul or spirit) or 3. As a symbol of what is external or 4. As the means of kindred or 5. (By implication) human nature (with its frailties (physically or morally) and its passions) or 6. (Specifically) a human being (as such): - carnal (-ly + -ly minded) flesh ([-ly]).

Since we are going to be talking a lot about our behavior, I'll primarily use definition number five for our purposes. From a Biblical standpoint, the flesh could also be defined as, the fallen, un-regenerated nature of our bodies. This is the extent of our human nature. This enemy is far more ruthless than Satan, because he only attacks us for a short while. Our flesh, however, is always with us. The only way to escape our flesh is to kill our bodies, which is not a viable solution. And while there is a limit to what Satan can do to us, our flesh, on the other hand, is only limited by our own imaginations. And our imaginations are only limited by what is possible in this world. In other words, "The sky is the limit".

The physical and spiritual worlds both operate by principle and by law. As human beings we are a part of both worlds.

We are souls with a spirit that makes us alive, which are part of the spiritual world. They are both housed in our body, which is governed by the physical world. Laws govern everything in this world from what is scientifically possible in nature to the interactions of people in polite society. The Apostle Paul in Romans chapter 7 begins to give us examples and comparisons of how laws even govern our human nature and our sense of morality.

The introduction of God's law actually strengthened the power of sin within us. This is true because sin automatically takes the opposite position of God's Law. The sin nature is diabolically opposed to God's law (Romans 7:8). So, when the commandment tells us, "Thou shalt not covet…" Then the law of the flesh which governs us, takes the opposite position and covets, simply because His Law says don't. Before we are born again, the law of the flesh completely controls us. There exists no other law to do otherwise, nor does there exist any other authority or power by which we may overcome the existing law that is in us.

Romans 7:18 – 21 For *I know that nothing good dwells in me, that is, in my flesh. For I have the desire to do what is right, but not the ability to carry it out. 19 For I do not do the good I want, but the evil that I do not want is what I keep on doing. 20 Now if I do what I do not want, it is no longer I who do it, but sin that dwells within me. 21 So I find it to be a law that when I want to do right, evil lies close at hand (ESV).*

In Paul's examination of himself, he has a revelation of where to find his enemy. He states that sin dwells in him. And if sin is in him, then the law of sin, which governs him, must be at work in him also (vs. 18). He knew that nothing good dwelt in his flesh. He desired to do the right thing but didn't know how, reasoning that he did not have the ability to do what was right. He lacked the ability because he was looking for it in the wrong place. It didn't exist where he was looking, which was in his flesh. It only exists in the spirit of a man that has been born again and regenerated by Christ. The goodness that Paul speaks of is not available in us at all, before salvation. The law of sin is the only thing that can manifest in us, because it's the only law that exists in us before we are born again.

I grew up in church and was taught that all you had to do was give your life to Jesus to be born again, and everything else would essentially take care of itself. That was not the specific statement, but it was the general idea. Therefore, I made an assumption, as so many Christians do, that because I had been born again and no longer desired to live a sinful life, that my sin issue had been eradicated. I assumed that once I learned what sin was (according to the Bible), and what God required of me through Jesus, I wouldn't have to ever worry about sin. It was now gone from my life. So imagine my surprise then, when, after not too long, I began to struggle with trying not to commit sin. Again, I made another assumption; common among believers, there was a lack of faithfulness, commitment, and devotion on my part that contributed to this struggle of mine. So, I would spend the next several years increasing my prayer, Bible reading, fasting, and church attendance. And while these disciplines certainly helped, and are an essential part of a believer's life, they did not make me immune to the desires and struggles of sin in my life. Well, you know what they say about assuming, right? And yet I made another common assumption. And this one was the most damaging one yet. It was the assumption that there was something abnormally wrong with me. I loved God, but couldn't seem to eliminate the issue of sin from my life, despite my best efforts. There's a lot to unpack in this statement, but for now I'm just going to deal with the reality of being born again and the law of sin residing in us.

Remember the only thing that can free one from a law is death. Romans 7:3-6 explains this point. A further example of this, is in ancient times when a king made a law of decree, it was binding, and could not be rescinded, not even by the king himself (See Dan. 6:7-16). That means the only way to get rid of the law of sin in our lives is for us to die. Which means that as long as we are alive, the law of sin still exists within us. Growing up, I was completely oblivious to this truth because no one had ever preached it or taught it to me this way. Being born again didn't get rid of my sin. It eradicated nothing. This raises the question, "What is the purpose of us being born again, if it is not to eliminate sin?" The answer is, to establish a greater and more powerful law within us. When we were born in this world the first time, we inherited the law of sin from our forefather Adam, when he sinned in the garden. When we are born again, we are born with a new law that is stronger and more powerful than the law of sin dwelling in us.

Let's deconstruct this internal battle of laws, so that we can truly understand our enemy and our warfare. Every man born after Adam is born with the law of the flesh and the law of sin in him. The law of the flesh is the fallen, un-regenerated nature of our bodies, or our human nature. The new law we receive is from Christ and is called the law of the Spirit. This new law supersedes both laws. Before we were born again, the only real choice we had, when it came to sin, was not if we would sin, but rather, what type of sin we would commit. Sin was inevitable. Because the laws of the flesh and sin were the only laws existing in us, we had no choice but to sin. There is the law of the mind that exists in us as well. This law is the law that goes head-to-head with the law of the flesh. However, the law of our mind is not strong enough to overcome the law of the flesh (Romans 7:23). We could refer to the law of the mind as our conscience. And for believers and non-believers alike, this is where the desire to do the right thing comes from once it has been properly guided and taught. This is why the secular world believes that man is inherently good, because of this desire to do right. However, merely the desire to do the right thing is not enough to actually make us righteous in God's eyes. Our conscience is no match against the raw desires of our flesh and our resolve inevitably loses the fight. Our minds are then taken prisoner and forced to labor under the law of sin. If we are not born again, then, death goes into effect. "Then when lust is conceived, it brings forth sin: and sin, when it is finished, brings forth death" (James 1:15).

This is why Christ says, "Come unto me, all you that labor and are heavy laden, and I will give you rest" (Matthew 11:28). He offers rest from the slave labor of sin. Therefore, what being born again really gives us, for the first time in our new lives, is a *real* choice between just having life and having life eternal. The choice now is not about how we sin, but how we choose to live.

With the introduction of the law of the Spirit, the law of our mind now has something to latch onto to pull it away from the clutches of the flesh. Our mind is now empowered by the Spirit to do the right thing. The right thing is found in the law of God: His Word. Christ stands at the door of our hearts to offer us salvation from the false choices we are given in this world which all lead to the same death. All roads do not lead to God. And all faith is not saving faith. Faith outside of Christ alone is merely designed to satisfy some aspect of our human nature and then get us to rationalize and justify our belief in a false path that leads to destruction.

I hope you noticed that there is no law mentioned here that gives Satan any right or power to make you do anything. He has to operate by law as well. The extent of his power is only manipulative and external, unless he is actually given permission to enter. This then, is demonic possession, and is a topic for another discussion. Satan is merely the master of suggestion. Since our flesh is tied to our bodies, and our bodies are tethered to this physical Earth, this then becomes his arena of operation. He inflames our flesh by making suggestions in our weakest area to get us to do things he cannot physically force us to do himself. If he can get us to fold, which is not that hard to do, this is exactly what he wants.

Make no mistake, however, we always have a choice of choosing between good and evil. The ability to choose is never taken away from us. As a matter of fact, God is not only the one presenting us with the choice, but He also helps us make the right choice. "See, I have set before you this day life and good, and death and evil;" (Deuteronomy 30:15).

Contrary to the popular "world view", there is a right and wrong choice. The good news is that God, in His infinite wisdom, mercy, and love, tells us the correct choice to make. "I call heaven and earth to record this day against you, that I have set before you, life and death, blessing and cursing: therefore choose life, that you and your seed may live:" (Deuteronomy 30:19). It's like taking an open book test. The answers are right in front of you. God says to us, "Choose life." Our soul or our mind now, has to choose between God's way and our way, and between His divine nature and our fallen human nature.

In the same way the law of the flesh joined forces with the law of sin, to bring our soul into bondage, the law of our mind joins with the law of the Spirit to conquer our flesh and sin and give us true freedom (Romans 7:25; 8:2). I pray this has cleared up any confusion you may have had, and answered some of your questions.

This may have no doubt stirred up other questions as it did for me. Are all these laws in operation simultaneously? Are we subject to two different sets of laws at the same time? Which laws govern, and when? To answer these questions that arose in my mind, I began to look at the governmental laws in my local area. I live in the northwestern portion of Indiana, right on Lake Michigan, about forty minutes from downtown Chicago. I used to work on the south side of Chicago while still living in Indiana. My commute was about thirty-five minutes every day, each way. I was running horribly late one day, so I was traveling the highway at a high rate of speed. I was about five minutes across the state line when I noticed a set of blue and red lights flashing in my rear view mirror. It was the Illinois State Police pulling me over. I pulled over to the shoulder of the road and got out my license and registration. The officer approached the window.

"Good morning, I need to see your license, registration, and insurance, please."

"Sure, officer", I said quickly, handing him my credentials.

"You were going pretty fast. Where are you headed?"

"To work."

"Let me guess. You're running late?"

"Yes sir."

"All right. I'll have to run your license. I'll be right back."

After a few minutes he came back to my window, with ticket in hand. He showed me on the ticket where I could go to pay it, and also showed me a website where I could pay it online. "Mr. Shelby, you have yourself a nice day, and please, slow down." And just like that, after about fifteen minutes, I was back on my way.

Both the state of Illinois and the state of Indiana have laws concerning highway speed. And even though I live in Indiana, I was stopped by an Illinois police officer and given a ticket. Why is that? The reason is because I was physically in the state of Illinois at the time of my infraction. Had I been speeding in Indiana, the Illinois officer would have had no jurisdiction whatsoever. Both states exist in one country, the United States. Both states' laws exist in each state simultaneously. However, I cannot be governed by both sets of laws at the same time, because it is impossible for me to be in both states at the same time. So, which set of laws governs me? Whichever state I happen to be in, that is the set of laws that I am governed by. When I am in Indiana, the laws of Indiana apply. When I am in Illinois the laws of Illinois govern me.

The same holds true for the spiritual state we find ourselves in. This is why the apostle Paul tells us not to walk according to the flesh, but according to the Spirit (Romans 8:5). Again, here is God through Paul, giving us the right answer. Walk in the Spirit, not in the flesh. Here's why. First, walking according to the flesh, results in death (vs 6). Second, we become enemies of God when we walk according to the flesh (vs 7). Thirdly, it is impossible to please God while walking according to the flesh (vs 8). The law that governs us is determined by where we walk. If we walk in the flesh, then the law of the flesh will govern. If we walk in the Spirit, however, then the law of the Spirit will apply. We have to choose where we walk, whether in the flesh or in the Spirit. Then God makes the choice easy by telling us the correct choice to make. "This I say then, walk in the Spirit, and you shall not fulfill the lust of the flesh" (Galatians 5:16 KJV).

.

CHAPTER 2
Enemy at the Gates

Guarding Your Mind at the Points of Entry

Could you imagine a wall around entire cities like Chicago, Los Angeles, New York, or Washington DC? It is hard to imagine anything like this in today's modern era, yet in ancient times this is exactly what cities did for protection. These walls that surrounded cities, fortresses, and garrisons had several gates in them. The gates had various functions from housing military supplies, food, commerce, livestock, waste removal, etc. What came in and out of the city, directly corresponded to the gate to which it was assigned. For example, dung and other waste removal was taken out through the "dung gate". Each gate was assigned a specific function, and only that function was accomplished through that assigned gate. These various gates also needed to be guarded to keep out bad elements that might gain access into the city. They were guarded against undesired entry of contraband, unsavory individuals, like thieves and murderers, and also against foreign invaders. Court cases and civil judgments were also decided at the gates, especially the main gate. Through these judgments the city was also protected against divisive ideologies and moral depravity that would undermine the wellbeing of the city.

Our souls are also like walled cities, housed within our bodies. And like those ancient cities, our souls have gateways that allow us to interact with the world. More importantly, those same gateways also allow the outside world to interact with *us*. And like those ancient gates, our own gateways need to be guarded against things that would kill, steal, and destroy. They need to be guarded against undesirable entry of contraband, the words of unsavory individuals, divisive ideologies, and moral depravities that would corrupt our souls. Christ fought the battle in his own body for our salvation. That battle has been won. However we do have a role to play in maintaining the freedom that has been won for us (Galatians 5:1). We must guard our gates and maintain the security of our souls so that we do not give our enemy (the flesh) the advantage over us.

I feel a need at this point to let you know that I am not a psychologist or a psychiatrist. I have no formal training on the subject matter. However, my observations of humanity and my study of the Bible, over the years, has led me to conclude that our souls are made up of two distinct parts. These two parts are our heart and our mind. Our heart is the seat of our emotions, personality, drive, and desire. Our mind is the seat of our reason, intellect, and will. The saying, "The heart wants what the heart wants" is a true statement, relatively speaking. How our emotions, drives, and desires behave, are not always based on rational thinking. And it is often difficult to explain why we feel the way we do, or why we want what we want. We will discuss this question later, but for now we will explore the need for gate security.

What are actually the gates to our souls? Any portal, through which we can give or receive concepts and ideas to or from the world around us, would be considered a gate. This would include our eyes, our ears, our mouths, and our imaginations. Our eye gate deals with ideas conveyed through images that we see. Internet, television, magazines, visual arts, and billboards are just a few of the mediums that send information through this gate. While the above mediums, in and of themselves are not bad, what we do with them can be. Pornography, violent or vulgar programming, gossip tabloids, and obscene art work are some examples of what we need to be on guard against when it comes to what we allow our eyes to see.

Our ears can receive ideas from these exact same mediums. Our ear gate deals with ideas and concepts conveyed through what we hear. Our eye gate and ear gate often receive information in tandem with one another. We are often listening to what we are viewing, or hearing what we read on the pages that are in front of us. So, not only can we receive "soul damaging" information from our eyes, but from our ears as well. And then there is our mouth. I'm sure everyone reading this would agree that our mouth can get us into a world of trouble. Because of the impact of what we say has on the rest of our lives, I would say that our mouth is the main gate. Just as the main gate was the seat of judgment and commerce in ancient times, so our mouth gate is to our souls and others around us. We pronounce judgment of good or bad, decree joy or mourning, declare blessings or cursing, all with the spoken word. There are so many passages in the Bible that have something to say about what we have to say. Here are just a few:

"Be not deceived, evil communications corrupt good manners" (I Corinthians 15:33 KJV).

"It is not what goes into the mouth that defiles a person, but what comes out of the mouth; this defiles a person" (Matthew 15:11 ESV).

"And the tongue is a fire, a world of iniquity. The tongue is so set among our members that it defiles the whole body, and sets on fire the course of nature; and it is set on fire by hell" (James 3:6 NKJV).

"...Who sharpen their tongue like a sword, and bend their bows to shoot their arrows- bitter words..." (Psalms 64:3 NKJV)

"Death and life are in the power of the tongue, and they that love it will eat its fruit" (Proverbs 18:21 NKJV).

Our mouth is a very powerful gate. So powerful in fact, that our very salvation comes through it, according to Romans 10:8-10. We confessed what we believed in our hearts and the result was the salvation of our souls.

Lastly, there is the gate of imagination. This gate is unique, in that it also is influenced and affected by the other three gates. What we see, hear, and say affects what goes in and out of our imagination. However, it also has the ability to conjure up its own concepts and ideas as if out of thin air.

These are thoughts that just come to our minds seemingly out of nowhere. But it is not out of "nowhere". It comes from somewhere. That somewhere is either our adversary Satan, or from the righteous or wicked recesses of our own hearts.

Our other enemy Satan waits to see if we will open our gate of imagination and receive the ungodly temptations he offers. The other place is from our hearts. Our hearts have deep places in them that we have carved out over time. We have carved out caverns especially for wicked devices and or grottos for righteous ideas and knowledge. These are the sources of holy and unholy thoughts and imaginations. The other gates, through what we see, hear, and say, help traffic the fuel to the fire that burns within our imagination gate. It is next to impossible to put out a fire that fuel is constantly being poured on. This is what we do when we allow all sorts of traffic through our gates. Many times our falling into sin has less to do with intentional disobedience and more to do with neglecting to be vigilant at the openings of our souls. "Be sober, be vigilant; because your adversary the devil walks about like a roaring lion, seeking whom he may devour (I Peter 5:8 NKJV). This neglect is often a result of watered down and weak doctrine. We are sometimes taught in many Christian circles that all we need to do is love Jesus and everything will be ok. We are rarely taught about our enemies and who they really are, that we have joined the ultimate fight of good vs. evil, or how we should behave during times of war.

Sometimes as believers, all we want to do is have fellowship dinners and sing songs around the campfire. Fellowship is good, but that cannot be the sum total of our faith, especially when we still have enemies to fight. I've had to learn this lesson the hard way. I learned it after years of suffering at the hands of an addiction from which I felt I would never be free. I had an unguarded gate that allowed this enemy to come and go as it pleased. Eventually it set up residence in my heart and became an addiction that I could not evict. Pornography ruled my life more than I realized and more than I was willing to admit. Because I was unaware just how dangerous lust was, I was unable to admit that there was even a problem. I viewed pornography as just a little thing. Because, that's how it started out in the beginning; it was just a little thing. I was told it was a normal adolescent behavior – a result of pubescent curiosity. It was an addiction. And it lasted well beyond my high school years. I had no idea that such "a little thing" would have such a big impact on my adult life. What I also, didn't know, was how strategic my enemy could be. Satan is strategic because he fights to win. We often fight just to get through the fight, or to just be left alone, so we can rest. He is well aware of this, so part of his strategy is patience. He waits until those moments we are at rest, and then sends temptation through that unlocked and unguarded gate. His hope is that his ally on the inside (our flesh) will do all the dirty fighting for him. And it does. This is how he gets us. This is how I was tripped up on many an occasion. With pornography, the more that came through my eye gates, the more I wanted to see. In other words, I dismissed the gate guards, busted the locks, and flung the gate wide open. And I still expected nothing bad to happen. What kind of protection is that? Many a believer is naïve in thinking that they can handle gate security on their own or, that they know best, what can and cannot go in or out of the gates. This is a huge strategic mistake. This is putting our flesh in charge of the gate, and the moment we do that, the security of our souls is compromised from the start. Our flesh will always compromise on what is evil.

I mentioned earlier that Satan is strategic. This means he's not stupid either. He's not going to bring a crate labeled "weapon of mass destruction", with a fully assembled weapon in it, to the front gate and expect it to get through. No. That's not his way. He rather brings small pieces and components of the weapon in, little by little, and over a period of time. The pieces don't look like a bomb at all. As a matter of fact, they look rather harmless and ordinary. He brings in a TV show and dirty joke here, and some gossip and a "white" lie there. And, before we know it, our flesh has assembled, piece by piece, a heart piercing missile that, when deployed, leaves our souls devastated. And we don't know we've been compromised until it blows up in our face. Our mind is reeling, our life is shattered, and we are left wondering "how did this happen?"

We must put our trust solely in the hands of Christ. For, He holds the responsibility to keep us from evil (II Thessalonians 3:3). Our job is to trust him. When we do, (and we must really do it; we can't fake this) then His job is to guard over us. (Philippians 4:7) We cannot assume His role and attempt to guard over ourselves, thinking that all of our spiritual disciplines (although necessary) are an adequate substitution for Christ Himself. This is salvation through works. Works not only keep us from eternal life, but also fail us in this present life, as well.

This was my mistake. And I suspect many believers' mistakes also. Our job is to guard what He has given us (I Timothy 6:20). And He has certainly given us salvation. But we are not to try to secure our own salvation or our own peace of mind, through religious works. Christ literally is our peace of mind (Ephesians 2:12-14a). When we have Christ, we have peace (Romans 5:1). And Christ's peace is also what sets us apart from sin and the world (I Thessalonians 5:23). We must understand that true peace is not the absence of conflict, but the serenity we have while going through it.

CHAPTER 3
Beware the Trojan Horse

Getting Inside the Strategy Behind the Warfare

There is a quote from a character in the 1995 movie, "The Usual Suspects" that says, "The greatest trick the Devil ever pulled was convincing the world he didn't exist." I have often thought to myself, "What about those who do believe in his existence?" I'm not exactly convinced that that's really his greatest trick, but it is a good one. I firmly believe that Satan has a menagerie of tricks at his disposal to use against various people groups and individuals alike. Satan has been fighting against us since we've been on this earth. He is an ancient foe and sometimes knows us better than we know ourselves. He is well acquainted with our nature and develops his strategy according to our desires, weaknesses, and tendencies. In other words, he's not just a one trick pony. And speaking of ponies, this puts me in mind of one of the most famous ancient war strategies that has ever been used. It is the story of the Trojan horse. Here's the short version for those of you who may not be familiar with the ancient account found in both the Latin poem the "Aeneid of Virgil" and Homer's "Odyssey". The story, according to the canonical version, is that there was a ten-year siege of the city of Troy by the Greeks during the Trojan War. The siege proved to be quite futile as Troy was a heavily fortified city. The Greek hero Odysseus came up with a plan to trick the Trojans with a fake tribute. The tribute was in the form of a giant wooden horse left at the main gate. The Greeks then pretended to sail away. The Trojans, seeing the tribute and believing that the Greeks had given up their siege of the city, opened the gates and pulled the horse in as a trophy. That day there was a grand victory celebration throughout the whole city. What the Trojans didn't know was that the horse was hollow, and hiding inside was forty of Greece's best warriors including Odysseus. Later that night the Grecian fleet sailed back under cover of darkness. And while the mostly drunken city continued to celebrate into the night, the Greek warriors climbed down out of the horse and opened the front gate. The Greek army decimated the city, thus ending the war.

Notice in the narrative that there wasn't anything the Greeks could do as long as Troy stayed behind the walls with the gates locked. It was Odysseus' clever scheme to entice Troy to open their own gates and let the enemy in. If Troy had only left the horse at the gate they would not have lost the war. This is exactly how Satan operates against us. He can't do anything against us as long as we stand behind God's Word with our gates locked. But somehow, using our frail human nature against us, he entices us to open our gates and let in his devices, which later end up doing us in. This is exactly what happened to me. Pornography was my Trojan horse. Yours may be something entirely different, but we all have one. It is something that has the ability to appear harmless and also tempt us to let down our guard and allow our enemy to walk right in. Remember, whatever gets past the gates, you will eventually have to fight. And it is far better to stop the enemy at the gates, than to have to fight him in the courtyard of your mind.

I stated earlier that, with pornography, the more I saw the more I wanted to see. It was my "drunken" celebration just before my downfall. A scripture that speaks of the Father's protection says, "...He will repay, fury to his adversaries, recompense to his enemies...So shall they fear the name of the Lord...When the enemy shall come in like a flood, the Spirit of the Lord shall lift up a standard against him" (Isaiah 59:18-19 KJV). In my celebrating, I managed to discard the Lord's standard, which is His Word, and cut off my lifeline of prayer. So when the enemy came in like a flood, I had no standard and it was next to impossible to close the gate amid the flood. I thought all I was doing was looking. But what I was really doing was arming my enemy with ammunition for the next phase of the attack.

If this first phase could be called "the set up", then this next phase could be known as "the entrapment". This is the phase where we learn just how entangled we really are, and how powerless and useless our struggling is. In the first phase, we might say something like, "I can quit, anytime I want." And at this point we may not even feel a need to quit. However, in this phase, we may realize that things may be starting to get a little out of hand. Our lifestyle may have begun to change in ways we never intended. It is now time to put the brakes on and put our money where our mouth is and pull back a bit. But then we realize that we can't. Every time the whim seems to strike, we are at its mercy. We can't stop when we want to. And now, we really want to. Two significant things usually happen in this phase. First, the carnal efforts we use to fight against the temptation ends up driving us to the point of exhaustion. We just get tired of fighting, tired of resisting, and tired of struggling. The second thing that happens is hopelessness and despair set in because our best efforts prove to be futile. The nature of the addiction ends up undermining our prayers and cries for help. We keep asking God to put out the fire, all while we are still pouring gasoline on it.

And after acres and acres of our souls have been scorched, then comes the final phase – "the takedown". Now, this is the time we get to watch everything we've built and all the things important to us get taken, or simply fall through our grasp. This is the slow downward spiral that now becomes painfully obvious to everyone around us. To those who are on the outside looking in, the downfall seems to have happened all of a sudden and extremely fast. They had no idea that the foundation of our lives was slowly being eroded from the inside. This erosion is so swift because the original breech puts in jeopardy the security of other gates. The devices and enemies that get in need support in order to survive behind the fortress of our heart. Therefore, other enemies are brought in through other gates. Lies, theft, deception, and evil communication come in to hide the tracks and help maintain the cover of the original enemy that breeched our walls. Often the symptoms are noticed but the root problem goes undetected. From the outside everything appears to be just fine. Appearances are kept up. Smiles and bright faces hide the true struggle of the soul. When asked, statements like, "I'm doing fine", or "I am blessed and highly favored", end up masking the real truth. And far too often, we are either too proud or too ashamed to ask for help from others. This pride and shame further solidifies "the takedown". Shame and pride serve to isolate us, and keep us suffering in silence until our utter destruction is complete. At this point, all that is left for us to do is to rummage through the broken fragments of our lives, wondering what, if anything, is left for us to salvage. It's not just desire for desire's sake. There is an end game to it all. The end game is our complete and utter destruction, and death.

James 1:13-15 *Let no one say when he is tempted, "I am being tempted by God," for God cannot be tempted by evil, and he himself tempts no one. (14) But each person is tempted when he is lured and enticed by his own desire. (15) Then desire when it has conceived gives birth to sin, and sin when it is fully grown brings forth death. (ESV).*

This is the end game, and it has to be stopped before it gets to the end. It never presents itself in an obvious way. At first, it's all about the fun, what we have been missing out on, or what we are able to gain. Temptation always falls into one of three categories. They are the desires of our flesh, the desires of our eyes, and the pride of living.

I John 2:15-17 *Do not love the world or the things in the world… (16) For all that is in the world – the lust of the flesh, the lust of the eyes, and the pride of life – is not of the Father but is of the world. (17) And the world is passing away, and the lust of it; but he who does the will of God abides forever. (NKJV)*

Satan tempted Eve in all three of these categories in the garden. "So when the woman saw that the tree was good for food, ("the desire of the flesh") that it was pleasant to the eyes, ("the desire of the eyes") and a tree desirable to make one wise, ("the pride of life") she took of its fruit and ate..." (Genesis 3:6 NKJV). He also tempted Christ in these after his fasting in the wilderness. "If you are the Son of God, command that these stones become bread" (the desire of the flesh). "If you are the Son of God, throw yourself down. For it is written 'He shall give His angels charge over you,'" (the pride of life). "...The devil took him up on an exceedingly high mountain, and showed Him all the kingdoms of the world and their glory..." (The desire of the eyes)(Matthew 4:3-11). We are tempted in these areas because these represent the areas that Satan can exploit our humanity – our basic primal needs. The desire of the flesh speaks to the temptation of our bodies – physical needs and desires. The desire of the eyes speaks to the temptation of our hearts – emotional needs and desires. The pride of life speaks to the temptation of our minds – intellectual needs and desires. In the previous chapter, I mentioned that we'd get back to why the heart wants what the heart wants and why our desires seem to run away with us. Well, the above is part of the reason why. The temptations target deficient areas within us – weaknesses. They were put there sometime in our past while we were still being developed. It was either in childhood, adolescence, young adulthood, or something some experience taught us.

For some of you reading this, this is a preview of what may come. To others this is a description of where you are right now. And to others still, this may be a painful reminder of the path that you have already walked. The good news is, that no matter where you might find yourself in this process, there is still hope. The hope is that as long as we are still breathing, it's not too late. Christ is always the solution to all the inequalities we have in our lives. "We have this hope as an anchor for the soul, firm and secure. It enters the inner sanctuary behind the curtain, where our forerunner Jesus, has entered on our behalf. He has become a high priest forever…" (Hebrews 6:19-20 NIV). We must always trust in Christ. "But the Lord is faithful. He will establish you and guard you against the evil one" (II Thessalonians 3:3 ESV).

We must remember not to attempt to guard our own gates, but must fully entrust that task to Christ. When our souls are secure, then we have peace. "...And the peace of God, which surpasses all understanding, will guard your hearts and minds through Christ Jesus." (Philippians 4:7 NKJV) Christ is not just a means to get peace; but He is our peace indeed (Ephesians 2:12-14a).

CHAPTER 4
The Bridge Is Out

Recognizing Warning Signs and Setting Healthy Boundaries

In the past few chapters, we have dealt with understanding our warfare, our defense, and our enemy. However, I feel a need to "switch gears" (pun intended) and change up my metaphors for this next illustration. Now days, it is next to impossible to travel anywhere in this country without coming across orange and white barrels. Yes, I'm talking about that dreaded road construction. There is that one orange and black "road construction ahead" sign that seems to make it depressingly official. There is nothing worse than trying to get somewhere only to have to take an inconvenient detour, or to be in a hurry, just to have four lanes of highway reduced to one. Road construction is inconvenient, frustrating, and irritating, to say the least. And I'm not saying that road rage is ok, but in the words of comedian Chris Rock, "I understand". So, if there just has to be road construction, at least the signs posted give ample warning and information about such things as speed, detours, lane usage, or whether or not the bridge is out.

This reminds me of a very tragic true story that occurred in my local area of Northwest Indiana. There is a small highway called Cline Ave. It serves as a main artery for the many steel mills and local refineries, as well as a link via the toll road to downtown Chicago across the border. In 2009, due to heavy truck traffic, steel haulers, and disrepair over the years, the section of highway that was a bridge was condemned. I still pass this section to this day. On March 28, 2015, an elderly couple, originally from Chicago, was following GPS coordinates and somehow accidently went off the condemned bridge. By the time the husband realized the bridge was out, it was too late. He slammed on the brakes, but not in time. He and his wife plunged nearly 40 feet to the ground below. The man, 64 years old, suffered a fractured spine, eye socket, and burns on his head, legs, and arms. He was able to exit the vehicle despite his injuries, before it was engulfed in flames. His wife, 51, was not able to escape, and was pronounced dead at a local hospital.

When I first heard the story, I was trying not to seem insensitive, but I remember thinking, "How is that even possible?" My question was due to my knowledge of all of the signage, traffic barrels, and wooden and concrete barricades he must have gone through. Regardless of what his GPS was telling him, he ignored a ton of visual cues in order to even make that tragedy possible. This is the sad inspiration for this chapter.

I began to think to myself, how we, as believers, make equally tragic decisions in our lives, because we fail to pay attention to visual, mental, and spiritual warning signs. The signs are always there, but we are not aware of them until we are sitting down in hindsight, after an apparent catastrophe.

The fact is, no one just happens to drive off the edge of an unfinished bridge. The same is true for some of the circumstances in which we find ourselves. We don't just happened to have an affair. We don't just happened to go bankrupt. We don't just happened to have unruly teenagers. We don't just happened to get divorced. Are you seeing the pattern here? There are many other situations and sins that we could substitute into the things that we could not have "just happened" to do. The reality is, like that couple on Cline Ave., we blew past a ton of detours, warning signs, and physical barriers to get into the situations we find ourselves.

We sometimes try to justify how we got there with statements like, "It's not like I meant to do it", "I don't know why I did that", or "That is so not like me". And still other times we just flat out blame someone else for our woes. "If God knew that I was going to fall, why did He let me get into this in the first place?" We even straddle the "blame" fence by blaming no one at all. "I'm only human, God understands and knows my heart." I cringe when I hear those statements.

God understands our humanity, but He doesn't excuse it when it comes to sin. And God most definitely knows our heart, and if we knew to what extent that He does, we wouldn't make this statement. He knows when we make those statements that we have no intention of changing our behavior at that time. He literally knows every excuse in the book and the ones that aren't even in the book as well.

Fortunately for us, we are not locked into these detrimental courses of action. We don't have to make bad choices. We don't have to sin. If we just learn how to recognize, understand, and adjust to the warning signs when we see them, we can avoid the consequences of catastrophe altogether. Let's start with recognition. This is rather difficult, because the enemy is subtle. Like I said earlier, he's not going to make it obvious. He's going to try to sneak it past the gates. But it is not impossible to spot, if we know what to look for.

First, know that sin is like a crime. In order for a crime to be committed, three things are needed, motive, means, and opportunity. Motive is the reason why a crime is committed. Means is the ability to commit the crime. And opportunity is the chance one has to actually do it. All three must be present in order for anyone to be convicted. In the same manner, we have to watch out for these things in our own lives.

We must be aware of our motives. Everyone has motives or reasons to sin. We may not all act on them, but everyone has them. Everyone. Remember, the heart wants what the heart wants. This by itself is not a bad thing, but we need to know what our desires are and their intensity levels. This is where temptation starts. I want ice cream – desire. I want five scoops of ice cream – intensity. Desire and intensity are the first areas for us to learn to recognize. Desire is not wrong, how we choose to satisfy that desire is what we need focus on. If we seek to satisfy our desire outside of the will of God, then we're in big trouble. Think about this the next time you try to rationalize your potential actions. How strongly do I want what I want? What does the Bible say about what I want? Is the process, by which I choose to satisfy my desire, pleasing to God?

The next area to watch out for is means – the ability to satisfy our desire. This goes beyond simply having money for purchases, a car to get to a destination, or a gun to fire at a target. Means, as it pertains to warning signs, is usually coupled with the motive for a potential result. For instance, being angry with someone and then realizing you have a gun tucked away in your closet is a dangerous warning sign. Those two items should never even be in the same thought let alone the same sentence. This example may seem extreme, but the process of temptation is the same, whether it is mild or severe. Means and motive are the two most dangerous to couple together. Because when these two come together and begin to fester in the mind, it is only a matter of time before the third one, opportunity, presents itself. This becomes the perfect storm of temptation, and I don't know anyone who can withstand its onslaught, without some divine intervention.

Opportunity is the final area to watch for warning signs. This one is also the most difficult because opportunity is so unpredictable. We have the least control over this area. We can't always predict when opportunity will arise. We can minimize it, but we can't see it coming 100% of the time. This is why we can never allow the coupling of motive and means. They can fester together for days, months, and even years. Then opportunity will choose a time most convenient for itself, and least convenient for us. "Of all the times, this had to happen now". Do you recognize that statement? We won't have to worry about this statement, if we keep a close eye on these three areas, and keep them separate from one another. I'll explain just how to do that in a moment.

Next, we need to have understanding of the process. How does this demise happen to us, and how does the enemy gain the advantage? As believers, we should never want to H.A.L.T. our forward progress in Christ. The reason is because it is much harder for our enemy to hit a moving target. You may be wondering why halt is spelled the way it is. It is actually an acronym for how we could be hindered in our walk. The dictionary definition of halt is as follows:

Halt (*verb*) *1. Bring or come to an abrupt stop (noun). 1. A suspension of movement or activity, typically a temporary one (verb). 2. Walk with a limp (adj.). 1. Lame* (Merriam-Webster dictionary).

Keep these definitions in mind as I explain the acronym. It stands for hungry, angry, lonely, and tired. And it represents the very emotions that we should avoid. If we allow ourselves to become too hungry, too angry, too lonely, or too tired, then we are "sitting" ducks, rather than soring eagles, for the enemy's attacks. Don't be too hungry. Hunger isn't necessarily the desire for food, although it includes food. It, rather, represents our sense of desperation in a circumstance or situation. Esau became too hungry (desperate) and ended up selling his birthright to Jacob for a pot of stew (Genesis 25:29–34). The Bible calls him a profane person for doing this (Hebrews 12:15-16). Don't be too angry. Anger without cause or justification is synonymous with murder and results in the same judgment (Matthew 5:21-22). Cain was too angry with his brother Able, and actually murdered him (Genesis 4:3-8). God cursed Cain to aimlessly wander the earth for the rest of his days (Genesis 4:10-12). Don't be too lonely. Loneliness not only refers to the absence of companionship, but despair and isolation as well. Jeremiah was too lonely (isolated and in despair) because of the nature of his message to Israel. He refused to preach God's message anymore and was depressed (Jeremiah 20:7-18). Don't be too tired. Job's wife was tired of suffering alongside her husband, as well as tired of seeing his health deteriorate. She lost faith and suggested he do the same (Job 1:13-22; 2:7-10). His wife is never mentioned again in the rest of the story, even when Job is restored in the end, along with all his belongings.

Do you remember the definition of halt? Metaphorically speaking, can you see how any one of these can bring us to an abrupt stop in life? When we are too hungry (desperate), angry, lonely (isolated and depressed), or tired, we are driven by raw desire and make irrational decisions that cause us to be lame and limp in our journey. God wants us to walk upright, straight, and steadily toward our goal.

Finally, once we recognize and understand our enemy's tactics, we must make the proper adjustments so that we can dodge his arrows, take away his advantage, and live in full victory. The first defense against the warning signs of sin is always the Word of God. So how do you keep the three areas of warning separate? We manage it by obeying God's Word. This is walking in the spirit. When we rely on our own understanding to navigate these areas, we actually lack the know-how, the ability, and the strength to do so. We become bogged down and stuck in our journey, unable to move forward. This is walking in the flesh. God's word always points us in the right direction. Here are some signs to follow from God's Word.

"Shun profane and idle babblings, for they will increase to more ungodliness" (II Timothy 2:16 NKJV). "But you, O man of God, flee these things and pursue righteousness, godliness, faith, love patience, gentleness" (I Timothy 6:11 NKJV). "Prove all things; hold fast to that which is good. Abstain from all appearance of evil" (I Thessalonians 5:22 KJV). "But understand this that in the last days there will come times of difficulty. For people will be lovers of self, lovers of money, proud, arrogant, abusive, disobedient to parents, ungrateful, unholy, heartless, unappeasable, slanderous, without self-control, brutal, not loving good, treacherous, reckless, swollen with conceit, lovers of pleasure rather than lovers of God, having an appearance of godliness, but denying its power. Avoid such people" (II Timothy 3:1-5 ESV).

Do you see the correct signs to follow? Notice the signs "shun", "flee", "pursue", "prove", "hold fast", "abstain", and "avoid". Many ignore signs like these, either because they feel that the consequences of the warnings won't happen or don't apply to them. People make statements like, "That's not going to happen to me", "I'm smarter than that guy was", or I know exactly when to back off". What they are really saying is that they are exempt from any effects, consequences, and judgments. The reality is they are not. It will come to them, and in a big way too. They will not have prepared themselves by making the proper adjustments. I implore you to make the necessary changes.

We need to stop living our lives by accident and start living our lives on purpose. Or rather, start living our lives with purpose. When we live our lives with purpose, we pay more attention to things; things like those small warning signs that we otherwise overlook. Our lives constantly have forces acting upon them, which require us to make conscious adjustments. Most of us are not as conscious of our lives as we should be.

Let's throw a little science into the mix. Part of Albert Einstein's theory of relativity states: an object in motion will stay in motion unless acted upon by some other force. We often think that our lives once set in motion, should remain on its course and everything will be just peachy. However, we fail to pay attention to the warning signs of those forces that can easily throw us off course. We don't make the adjustments to the forces that push against our lives. The result is that our life is pushed ever so slightly off course. String enough of these little pushes together and we may find that our life is so far from where we intended it to be. The good news is we can use the Word of God to make the proper course corrections. Having faith in Christ means obeying His Word. We need to walk in the spirit. Obey His Word. And allow Him to order our steps and get us where we need to be.

CHAPTER 5
Flesh Versus Flesh?

Choosing the Right Weapons to Win Against the Enemy

I have discovered that our society is a uniquely tailored environment for our adversaries' advantage in this war. We have social media links, news and entertainment outlets, communication hubs, and satellite networks. Never before have we been so instantly and readily connected to one another, and so hopelessly isolated from one another at the same time. This plays into Satan's strategy to divide and conquer.

This current cultural fishbowl, we call America, has over the course of time, stripped us of the concept of dependency on community and neighbors, and to some extent, friends and family. Over the years, our families have become numerically smaller, while at the same time having a smaller influence over our ideologies, our moralities, and our values. We've been somewhat distanced from family and friends, living at far ends of the country, pursuing employment opportunities and the promise of a better life. Because of this separation, we've been forced to become self-reliant and self-sufficient. In this culture, it's become necessary for survival.

Though this may be true for most of America, you might ask yourself, how this truth plays into this warfare scenario we've been talking about all this time. It is actually a tactic of conditioning from Satan, launched against the masses. He uses this tactic against those of us who could potentially become his adversaries, through faith in Christ. The reason is so that we have a defeated mindset, before we even set foot onto the battlefield. He uses the lies of this current cultural climate, to promote self-reliance and self-sufficiency. These ideas penetrate our ears and imaginations at extremely early ages.

First, he uses the lie of self-reliance (the belief that all we need to succeed at anything in life is ourselves and our determined mindsets). The next lie he uses is self-sufficiency (the belief that we alone have the ability to catapult ourselves into the successes of life). While it is true, that we do play a big part in our own success, in the words of 17th century poet John Donne, "No man is an island."

In this warfare, we cannot, under any circumstances, rely on ourselves to fight these battles. Think about this. There is no army in the world that would ever expect its enemies to bomb their own facilities, blow up their own arsenal, or shoot their own troops. Your thoughts in reading that statement might be something like, "No kidding, Captain Obvious!" However, when it comes to battling our own inner "demons", we rely on ourselves to get the job done. We fail to realize that, our inner selves and our inner "demons" are quite often one and the same. Our inner "demons", most of the time, are just manifestations of a damaged and dysfunctional heart. We are literally our own worst enemy. And most of the time, we figure this out far too late, if we ever figure it out at all. We cannot fight ourselves and expect to win. I'm going to just let that sit and marinate for a while. Because, I believe many of us think that we can. Let me assure you, we cannot. It is like trying to play chess against yourself. The question is who wins and who loses? It is often believed that to win any battle we must fight fire with fire. But this is what pitting our inner "demons" against our inner selves actually is. And what we are left with are two burned down forts and the stench of a scorched soul.

You cannot combat the body's fallen nature with weapons that require that same nature to be used against itself. The law of self-preservation kicks in. You cannot expect your body to participate in harming itself. This includes its nature. This is the inherent weakness or limitation of the law, according to Romans 8:3. The Law of God is designed to identify and point out our sin, not save us from it. As far as the Law is concerned, it expected humanity's full obedience, regardless of the fact that we neither had the power nor the ability within us to do it.

This is what Paul meant in Romans 7:18 (KJV) about not finding the "how" to perform that which was good. It didn't exist in him. It was never there to begin with. He was both surprised and disappointed by this very fact, as are most people today, and more so. More so, because in today's society, the common thought is that, man, at his core, is inherently good and happens to do a few bad things every now and then. This is in direct contradiction from what Romans 7:18 teaches when Paul tells us that there is nothing good that resides in his flesh. The reality of man is that we are, in our fallen nature, inherently bad, and we manage to do some good things from time to time.

This false view of the goodness of man's heart is the fatal flaw and undoing of many believers and unbelievers alike. It is fatal in the sense that this misplaced trust has killed many marriages and friendships. This false assumption has undone many, by keeping us in a vicious cycle of self-reliance that deceives us at every decision juncture. It is often said, when we are faced with a difficult decision, "Just trust your heart". This is one of the most dangerous statements there is. The Bible tells us what's wrong with our hearts from the beginning. "The heart is deceitful above all things, and desperately wicked: who can know it" (Jeremiah 17:9 KJV)? According to the scriptures, we can characterize our hearts as deceiving, wicked, and mysterious. It is deceiving because it is unreliable. If you recall, earlier we talked about how the heart is the seat of our emotions, desires, and drives. These things are fickle and subject to change with the wind of each circumstance and situation. Therefore our hearts are fickle as well, and can't be trusted. If our hearts unknowingly deceive us, and it is a common practice to "Just trust your heart", then how well is our self-reliance serving us? I would say, without Christ, not well at all.

Here is fair warning. This next one is going to hurt a bit,

because the truth often does. Our hearts are wicked. There.
I said it. Now, I can already hear some of you out there
saying, "Well, I'm not that bad". Well, we're not that good
either. In fact, we're nowhere near as good as we think we
are. I'll prove it to you. How many times, have we been
wronged by someone, and given a Biblical response the first
time out? And for those of you who feel that you have
passed this question with flying colors, here's a follow up
question. How many times have you told someone off or
cursed someone out in your head over similar
circumstances? See, that's just one scenario. There are
countless others that play out for us on a daily basis, in
exactly this same way. We either physically give an
unbiblical response, or we think about one. In God's eyes,
thinking it is just as bad. Remember what Christ said to the
Pharisees in the book of Matthew. "You have heard that it
was said, you shall not commit adultery.' But I say to you
that everyone who looks at a woman with lustful intent has
already committed adultery with her in his heart"
(Matthew 5:27-28 ESV). Committing adultery is the physical

sin, but notice where the other offense was committed. That's right. It was in the heart.

The last flaw of our heart is that it is full of mystery. Jeremiah asks, "Who can know it?" We have a whole field of study dedicated to the exploration of the soul. Psychiatry, psychology, sociology, and psychotherapy have made great strides in this area. But for all their expertise, there are still things of the soul that cannot be explained. There are mass shootings, riots, suicides, drug epidemics, child molestations, etc., and the experts struggle to find plausible explanations for any of them. The fact of the matter is, "the heart wants what the heart wants", and we don't really know why. When something is broken and you don't know exactly how it's put together or how to fix it, the best thing to do is to call the manufacturer. The manufacturer has the specs on how it's put together, knows the common problems that often arise, and has the genuine parts to replace or repair any defect. Since we don't really know what we're doing when it comes to our hearts, we need to refer to the manufacturer. This takes all of the mystery and guesswork out of the equation, and simplifies our lives beyond compare.

God has all of the specifications of our hearts. "I praise you, for I am fearfully and wonderfully made. Wonderful are your works; my soul knows it very well. My frame was not hidden from you, when I was being made in secret, intricately woven in the depths of the earth. Your eyes saw my unformed substance; in your book were written, every one of them, the days that were formed for me, when as yet there was none of them" (Psalms 139:14-16 ESV). God is well acquainted with the problems and mysteries of our heart. "If we had forgotten the name of our God or spread out our hands to a foreign god, would not God discover this? For he knows the secrets of the heart" (Psalms 44:20-21 ESV). God has the genuine parts to replace and repair the defects of our heart. "And I will give them singleness of heart and put a new spirit within them. I will take away their stony, stubborn heart and give them a tender, responsive heart" (Ezekiel

11:19 NLT).

Remember, we cannot fight our flesh by using our flesh. Don't fight fire with fire. It won't work. Instead, fight fire with an inferno. The fire of the flesh is no match against the inferno of the Holy Spirit. John answered, saying to all, "I indeed baptize you with water; but one mightier than I is coming, whose sandal strap I am not worthy to loose. He will baptize you with the Holy Spirit and fire. His winnowing fan is in His hand, and He will thoroughly clean out His threshing floor, and gather the wheat into His barn; but the chaff He will burn with unquenchable fire" (Luke 3:16-17 NKJV). The chaff of the flesh is burned away. And what is left is a new, clean heart, purified by faith (Acts 15:8-9).

CHAPTER 6
Avoid the Void

An Idle Mind Truly Is the Devil's Workshop

There is one country in the world that has managed to stay out of every major conflict and war for over the last 200 years. This country has been so successful at being neutral, that it has literally become famous for it. If you haven't guessed the country by now, I'm referring to Switzerland. This avoidance of war seems, for the most part, to have served the Swiss well.

However, when it comes to spiritual warfare, there is no such thing as neutrality. We have to make a choice as to which side we're going to be on (Deuteronomy 11:26-28; 30:19, Joshua 24:15). Some people are so confused or apathetic about the choice that they decline to make one. They want to be like Switzerland. They want to be left alone. And this self-preserving concept would be just fine except for the fact that it actually preserves nothing. Our peace of mind isn't preserved, because Satan makes sure we're pulled into the fray even when we're not bothering him. Our way of life isn't preserved, because we will have to deal with the struggle of sin and its consequences. And our afterlife certainly isn't preserved, because without our belief in and confession of Christ, we cannot be saved. Therefore, not making a choice is actually a choice in itself.

Though even after we have chosen Christ, many of us still struggle with sin. If any of you are anything like me, you're probably wondering how this is even possible. This is only possible if we are not making the right choices when it comes to temptation. The same choice we made when we became born again, is the same choice we have to make every day when temptation comes. The water of our choices becomes muddy because we're not exactly sure how we feel about the sin to which we are tempted. We just have to be honest. The temptations that we are faced with are either physically beneficial, stroke our ego in some way, or are just downright fun. Remember the categories, the lust of the flesh, the lust of the eye, and the pride of life.

As believers, we don't want to admit that we sometimes like the sin and its temptation. We want to believe that our love for God won't allow us to be affected by it. Or, that our spiritual disciplines alone will bail us out of how we feel. But, we are actually being dishonest with ourselves. If we are dishonest with ourselves, we cannot even recognize the danger that we're in, let alone, be able to ask for help to get out of it. This dishonesty causes us to become indecisive or double-minded, if you will. This double-mindedness, in turn, paralyzes our ability to make a choice in those subsequent, crucial moments. We yearn to be like Switzerland. We don't want to make a choice. So, we defer, trying to buy ourselves some time while we figure it out. However, in the fleeting moments that we purchased with our deferment, we don't actually figure anything out at all. We have often used that time to give our minds respite from the pressure, and end up ignoring the decision altogether. That is until the next wave of temptation comes with more intensity and magnitude than before. And if we hadn't settled the issue before, we're not likely to do so in those next more intense moments. Our only options at that point seem to be to defer yet again or fold.

Our deferment, however, only serves to strengthen the pull of sin within us, rather than arming us so that we can fight against it. It does this in two ways. First, this deferment gives us some time. But it also gives the enemy time. And the amount of time I'm talking about isn't necessarily a week or a day. It can be as little as ten to fifteen minutes of indecision, which gives the enemy just enough room to get his foot in the door, in order to manipulate our decision-making process. We use this time as a means to alleviate the pressure and allow our minds to check out for a bit. The enemy uses this time to lull our sensibilities, so we are less likely to put up a fight when the next round of temptations come. This lull is almost hypnotic. And as any hypnosis expert will tell you, an empty or clear mind is an optimal environment for hypnotic, or in this case, spiritual suggestion. Satan uses our flesh to spiritually hypnotize our minds so we no longer have the ability to resist sin. Second, our deferment, due to our indecisiveness, creates a type of void or vacuum in our minds, where our determination should be. Scientifically speaking, anytime there is a vacuum in nature, it must be filled. A vacuum involving fire is called a backdraft. A vacuum of heat in the atmosphere results in a cold front. And a vacuum of cold produces a warm front. Likewise, a soul, devoid of righteous occupation, eventually becomes filled with sin.

So, the question is, how do we combat the enemy and avoid the void? Before we can answer that question directly, let me ask you another question first. Have you ever gotten a song that you didn't like stuck in your head? Ever try not singing or humming that particular tune? Yeah. It's extremely difficult, isn't it? You keep beating your palm against your forehead, telling yourself, "I'm not gonna sing that song! I'm not gonna sing that song!" The only thing is, thirty seconds later, you find yourself singing that song. I find that the best way to get rid of an unwanted tune is not to "try not to sing that song", but rather, sing a different song, altogether. We get so involved with singing the new song, that it puts the old song right out of our minds. This is something I like to call replacement therapy. Replace the old with new. All of a sudden, getting rid of the old is not as difficult. As believers, we often make this same mistake. We pound our palms against our foreheads, and repeat to ourselves, "Don't dwell on the temptation. Don't dwell on the temptation." The only problem is, moments later, all we can think about is that temptation. The concept of replacement therapy is actually in the Bible.

"Finally, brothers, whatever is true, whatever is honorable, whatever is just, whatever is pure, whatever is lovely, whatever is commendable, if there is any excellence, if there is anything worthy of praise, think about these things. What you have learned and received and heard and seen in me—

practice these things, and the God of peace will be with you" (Philippians 4:8-9 ESV).

The Apostle Paul isn't simply telling us not to think evil thoughts, but rather what type of thoughts we should be thinking. It is a replacement of the evil, with the good. And he is not telling us to only think of the good, but verse 9 tells us to "practice these things" as well. The combination of believing the right things in the mind, along with the outward performance of those beliefs, results in a relationship with the God of peace. This is the essence of saving faith according to Romans 10:9-10. There is a belief in the heart and an outward confession of the mouth that produces true salvation. Believing in the Lamb of God, who is Christ, and looking to Him in our moments of weakness, causes our void to be filled with the Father of peace. This gives us the greatest weapon we could ever have to fight temptation with, the Father Himself. He, in turn, fights for us.

CHAPTER 7
A Ban on Boomerangs

Battling the Things That Keep Coming Back Around

In Australia, there is an ancient device that was developed, long ago, by the Aboriginal people, called a boomerang. Made of smooth wood, and often V or L shaped, it was tapered like an airplane wing at both ends, giving an aerodynamic design to it. A warrior would throw the boomerang away from himself, into the air, with a flick of his wrist. The boomerang would then spin as it flew through the air. While in flight, its course begins to alter and travel in a circular trajectory; looping around right back to the warrior that threw it.

Settlers who saw this for the first time, often tried to throw one themselves to duplicate this phenomenon of flight, with less than stellar results. The boomerang holds a secret. And it is not visible to the naked eye. The secret to the way a boomerang works is actually in how it's released. As the warrior throws the boomerang, the flick of his wrist causes it to spin. As it spins, one end begins to spin faster than the other. This creates imbalance and instability as it slices through the air. This causes the air mass around the boomerang to also become imbalanced, pushing it off course and looping it back around to its starting position. It is actually the imbalance that causes the boomerang to move the way it does.

As I looked at how a boomerang responds, I thought, this is often how people behave in life. And just like the secret of the boomerang, the "why" behind our trajectory in life is not always visible to others, or to us, for that matter. Why we behave the way that we do, contradicting God's Word, is most times, due to how we start; the release. Like the boomerang, we either get ahead of ourselves in one area of our lives (this is the part that spins faster than the rest), or we're lagging behind and underdeveloped in an area, (this part spins slower than the rest). This is where the imbalance comes into effect. It is the imbalance that causes us to wobble off our intended course. This imbalance creates turbulence, bringing our lives out of balance, and causing the forces of life to push back against us, taking us where we didn't intend to go. Incidentally, the more we go forward, the more we find ourselves circling right back to where we started.

In the cases where we get ahead of ourselves, we become too anxious, too impatient, or too greedy in our ambitions. In the cases where we are lagging behind or are underdeveloped, we have become too afraid, too complacent, or have too low self-esteem. Either way, both scenarios will cause us not to progress in life beyond the place of our imbalance.

Let's not get ahead of ourselves. If we are able to be honest with ourselves, we can admit there have been things we've gone through in our past that we did not get through gracefully, and the thought of ever going through it again is enough to make our hands sweat, our breath shorten, and our hearts forget what beat it's on. This is classic anxiety. Not to be confused with anxiety disorder, which is a medical condition. I'm talking about your run-of-the-mill, good old fashioned, everyday "worry". The perspective of this worry, for some of us, has its foundation deeply rooted in our past.

Anx-i-e-ty *(noun) a* feeling of worry, nervousness, or unease, typically about an imminent event or something with an uncertain outcome. *He felt a surge of anxiety.*
Synonyms: worry, concern, uneasiness, unease, fearfulness, fear, disquiet, disquietude, inquietude, perturbation, agitation, angst, nervousness, nerves, tension, tenseness, etc. A desire to do something, typically accompanied by unease. *The housekeeper had an eager anxiety to please.*
Synonyms: eagerness, keenness, desire; an anxiety to please.

I'm going to pull from both definitions, particularly the second one. The reason being, it lends itself to action, i.e. getting ahead of ourselves. Earlier, I mentioned the perspective of our worry. Perspective is as unique as your fingerprint, and it

BATTLING THE ENEMY WITHIN

is based on the vantage point from which you witnessed something. If ten people witnessed an accident, there would probably be ten different eyewitness accounts of that very same accident. There'd be ten different perspectives, because there were ten different positions from which people saw the accident.

From the standpoint of our past, our unique vantage point is based on our state of mind, our maturity level, our emotional state, and our belief system about and during the event, just to name a few. If we then can have an incomplete, unhealthy, or distorted perspective shaped by our past, then it stands to reason, that our perspective would be equally skewed, moving forward. So then, what's the answer? How do we undo the damage done to us in our past? The answer, as always, is found in God's Word.

Philippians 4:6-7 *NKJV*

6 Be anxious for nothing, but in everything by prayer and supplication, with thanksgiving, let your requests be made known to God;

7 and the peace of God, which surpasses all understanding, will guard your hearts and minds through Christ Jesus ESV.

The apostle Paul clearly tells us *not* to be anxious, and **how** and **what** to do about our anxiety in vs. 6, then tells **why** and more importantly, **who,** in vs. 7. Let's look at the how. Our anxieties are quelled by prayer, supplication, and thanksgiving. Prayer, simply put, is our communication to God of our petition, intercession (petition on behalf of others), thankfulness, praise, and repentance. Our prayer falls into one of those categories. If prayer is our communication to God, then supplication is *how* we communicate, or our approach. We approach Him humbly as God, because He is. We approach Him reverently as creator and as a king, because He is both. And we approach Him earnestly as one having great authority, because He has all authority and ability to do what we ask. Now we can look at the what. The "what" is the easy part. It is the actual request. It's the action we want God to take for us.

Another word for anxiety is simply fear. Fear is such a subtle and unassuming thing at first. It makes us believe that by ignoring it, that we have gotten over it, when in actuality, it has released us into a wobbly life altering course of turbulence and imbalance that baffles our sense of direction and leaves us wondering what went wrong. Fear may be subtle at first, but it grows up, right along with us. And before long, it becomes a monster that destroys our focus, demands that we cower to it, and causes us to behave in all sorts of irrational ways.

Fear destroys our focus by distorting our perspective. We need our perspective to focus. It's how we view things. But if our perspective is off, then our goals never come into sight. We don't end up where we intended to go, and we don't accomplish what we set out to do. How does this insignificant seed of fear that starts out so small, end up so

big and control us so much. It's simple. We fed it. Our
enemy caused us to focus on our fear, rather than where we
were going, what we were doing, and more importantly, the
answer and solution to keep us on course.

I remember, as a kid, having to take a weeklong series of
standardized tests one year. My sisters and I spent the
weekend at my grandparent's house, right before testing
started that Monday. I spent Sunday afternoon with my uncle
watching a horror movie marathon of the old black and white
monster movies. We watched various Dracula movies, a
couple of different Mummy movies, a werewolf show, and I
think an alien movie was thrown in for good measure. It was
dark when my parents came to pick us up. "Alright, straight
to bed now, you've got school in the morning. "No problem, I
went right in and got ready for bed. Now if you had asked me
back then, "Do you believe in monsters, ghosts, or aliens", I
would have told you, "No way!" And I didn't believe in that
stuff, except that night, for some reason, was different. What
I thought I believed didn't matter anymore. My sensibilities

went right out the window.

That night I didn't fall asleep, right away, like I usually did. My parents went up to bed. My sisters shared a room, and their conversation faded away as they drifted off to sleep. If you had been there in the house, you'd have said that all was quiet. And it was, but not to me. My window was open, so I could hear the wind rustling through the trees, just like in that Dracula movie. My curtains swayed in the breeze. The moonlight played around with the shadows of the keepsakes and trophies I had on my dresser. Every sound seemed to be magnified. I heard the crickets outside my window. The settling of the house was unnerving. Normally, it would've been no big deal for my closet door to be open, except this night the light from the other window was cascading down something very dark and ominous just on the other side of the door. The shadows seemed to move and shift as the hours went by. Yes, you read correctly, I said hours, with an s. I was up all night. The last time that I looked at my clock, it read 5:08 am. I was jarred from my snooze by my alarm, with it flashing 6:00 am. I was up the entire night, and slept less than an hour, over fear of things that I knew weren't real and didn't exist. Now how irrational was that? Obviously I wasn't seeing things clearly. My perspective was off. My perspective was not looking through the understanding of what I knew to be true, but through the lens of my fear.

It is easy to get caught up in the moment, and focus only on the fear that stands before us, instead of the understanding of the truth that we know. We have to be careful not to focus on the wrong thing that leads us to become too anxious. However, we can be focused on the right thing so intently, that we outrun our spiritual and personal development. Being too impatient is another way for us to get ahead of ourselves and cause imbalance. We get ahead of ourselves without even knowing that that's what's happening to us at the time. Our distorted perspective will often cause us not to recognize what our Heavenly Father is doing in our lives. And if we cannot recognize the move of God to do us good, then we will also, most often, misidentify His provision, His timing, and His blessings when they manifest themselves to us. This can cause us to inadvertently work against the very things we've been praying for.

According to Genesis 8:22, The Most High established a natural law, and a spiritual principle that are both in effect to this day. It is simply that the cycles of the seasons, seedtime and harvest, and summer and winter, would continue, as long as the Earth remained.

Genesis 8:22

While the earth remaineth, seedtime and harvest, and cold and heat, and summer and winter, and day and night shall not cease (KJV).

There are two seasons mentioned by name, and they are summer and winter. The other two are identified according to their function, which are seedtime and harvest, and represent the movement or transition of time into the other seasons. Looking at this passage about "seedtime and harvest", most of us do understand that there is a transition of time between the seed and the harvest. While examining all the components of these two seasons, we can come to understand them through their most important elements, which are the seed, time, and the harvest. We need to have the correct understanding of the purpose of all three, because if we don't, we could be left to wobble off course never reaching our full potential or arriving at our intended goal.

If we misunderstand the seed and see it only as food to be eaten, we tend to consume it all, and we then have nothing left to plant. Therefore, we can expect to receive no harvest. We must recognize that the seed is a potential harvest. If we misunderstand time, and view it either as something to be painstakingly endured, or ignored altogether, then we mismanage our time, and reap too soon or reap too late, and end up with very little to no harvest at all. We must recognize that time is the process of maturing the seed into harvest. If we misunderstand the harvest, and see it only as a reward for all of our hard work, then we tend to consume the harvest as we please. We are then left wanting and depleted of seed for the next season of seedtime. We must recognize that *this* harvest is also seed for our *next* harvest.

The seed is the provision of God (Isaiah 55:10). Time is the process of God (Genesis 4:3, Joel 2:23-24, and Jeremiah 5:24). The harvest is the promise of God's blessing (II Corinthians 9:10). But we must go beyond mere recognition to get to the very power of the revelation itself, or rather, Himself. Christ is the power behind the seed, the time, and the harvest. He is the one who stabilizes our imbalances, calms the turbulence, and steadies our wobble, so we can straighten up and fly right.

He is our provision, because He is the seed (Galatians 3:16). We must remember that it is not our job, or our business, or the stock market, or our friends, or our family that are our provision. Christ is our source and true provision, because He is the one that actually supplies our job, our business, the market, and our friends and family. Whether they know it or not, they all are dependent on Him for *their* provision as well.

And while we are anxious about time, time is of no consequence to the one who is eternal and is "The Ancient of Days". He is able to "restore to [us] the years" that have been eaten away, and that we seemingly have wasted (Joel 2:25). He is the master of time, because He created time (Genesis 1:14). He holds the timelines of our lives firmly in His hands, and He considers our failures and our immature deadlines right along with it. We are able to fail miserably, and be blessed abundantly, all in the same timeline, because He "[declares] the end from the beginning", all while viewing our entire timeline in just one glance (Isaiah 46:10). And we try to declare our own destiny, and we cannot see past the next minute. We need to repent of the sin of self-reliance, which is idolatry (I Samuel 15:23). He alone is able to take all of the guesswork out of our path (Psalm 5:8; 27:11). And if we will learn to trust Him in our journey, He is able to get us to the destination that both He and we want to end up (Philippians 1:6). And when we get to that destination, we need not worry about what we will have to show for it, when it's all said and done, (Mark 10:29-30) or whether or not there will be anything waiting at all (Romans 4:21) Christ *is* our harvest. (John 15:5) He is able to give us an abundant harvest, because He is The Lord over the harvest. The harvest is in only His power to give (Matthew 9:38, Luke 10:12). The promises come only through Him.

However, we must have the right motive. It has become part of the culture of today's modern Christianity, to desire the harvest, simply for the sake of having the harvest. Desire is a powerful thing. It is part of the life force that we have inside of us. And it motivates and propels us forward toward our goals and destiny. Desire, is also the destructive force behind our greatest depravity and basest nature. Desire itself is not evil. What determines whether our desire is good or whether it is evil, is how we choose to satisfy that desire, and in what quantity. For example, there is nothing evil about hunger, however, gluttony is a different matter altogether.

Sleep is good for the body. But sloth, on the other hand, yields no productivity whatsoever.

Greed is one such desire that, by its nature, has been subjected to twisting and distortion. It is a desire that pulls way too much, and hangs on far too long. It is certain to get us off course and wobbling out of control in a hurry. By definition, greed is a desire for more than what is needed (Luke 12:18). It is also a desire for more than what is ours or what belongs to us (Exodus 20:17). We are able to do a fairly good job at defining what greed is, but recognizing it in our own lives, for what it really is, is far more difficult.

Greed hides exceptionally well. Greed shrouds itself underneath our rationalizations and justifications. Therefore, it does not look like greed at all. Greed walks around masked behind our reasons, in order to appear legitimate. It is a false need that has been generated, in order to avoid detection. How then do we pull the cover off of our greed, and expose it for the monster that it is?

Well, sometimes when we can't seem to *see* greed's presence, we *are* able to *hear* its voice when it speaks. It may sound something like this. "I work a lot of hours to provide for my family". The truth may be that we work a lot of hours to support a lifestyle to which we feel entitled. You know, it is sort of like that promise we made to ourselves a long time ago. We may have said, "Never again", or "One of these days, I'm going to have that". It seems legit. It seems reasonable. And when the average person hears those statements, they often sympathize and agree with them. The behavior is excused because, there are mitigating circumstances of the past and it's totally understandable. The scripture tells us that man looks on the outer appearance, but that God looks at our hearts. What, may be excused by man, is not so easily dismissed by God.

Greed is extremely dangerous, it can get us so far off course, so very quickly. If we ever do realize that we *are* off course, our surroundings are so unfamiliar and unrecognizable, that we may abandon all hope and abort our very destiny.

Duty may be one mask that greed wears, but sometimes, ambition can be an equally concealing cloak of this stealthy evil. It may sound like this, "God wants us to be successful and blessed", or "What's wrong with having nice things"? On the surface these sound like legitimate statements and questions, however, these are often just facades with greed as a shady backstory. We have to be careful not to twist or pull scripture out of its context when using this line of reasoning. Here are a few statements and scriptures to remember to help guard our minds against poor perspectives that we may have picked up along the way. Greed always ignores the responsibility that comes along with being blessed, and casts a shadow on one's profession of faith.

I John 3:17 *But whoso hath this world's good, and seeth his brother have need, and shutteth up his bowels of compassion from him, how dwelleth the love of God in him?*

No matter how hard you look, true blessing does not have a down side.

Proverbs 10:22 *The blessing of the Lord, it maketh rich, and he addeth no sorrow with it.*

If we have no purpose for the acquisition of worldly possessions, then we consent to our transformation into fools.

Luke 12:18-20 *And he said, this will I do: I will pull down my barns, and build greater; and there will I bestow all my fruits and my goods. And I will say to my soul, Soul, thou hast much goods laid up for many years; take thine ease, eat, drink, and be merry. But God said unto him, Thou fool, this night thy soul shall be required of thee: then whose shall those things be, which thou hast provided?*

All success is not equal (Joshua 1:8). If Joshua refers to the success in this passage, as *good* success, then, it stands to reason, there is such a thing as *bad* success as well. There is the kind of success that is so linear in its pursuit of its goal, that it fails to include the other things in life that are essential for the enjoyment of that goal, once it has been achieved. For example, a man works many hours to provide a high-end home and luxury car, in a ritzy neighborhood, for his wife and children. However if he spends no time with them as a husband or as a father, he may have the house and the car, but lose the family for which he worked so hard to provide. There would be no one left with whom to enjoy his success. Can you see how greed could have driven him to succeed with so much focus and tunnel vision that it could cause him to lose sight of what was really important in his life? Has greed been hiding in the recesses and crevices of your own life? How's that for a boomerang effect? The imbalance of greed can cause us to lose everything and have us start from square one.

Greed is selfish and self-serving. So, when it comes to escaping the grip of greed, square one is not necessarily a bad place to be. God has a way of allowing circumstances, in His own timing, to bring us to that very place. He does this to get us to realize the condition of our own heart, and that what we really need is Christ.

In the Gospels, Christ often pronounced woe or judgment on those who were rich (Matthew 6:24-25); not because they were wealthy, but because they had not lived up to the responsibility of their riches (Matthew 25:42, James 1:27) We cannot seek after things apart from Christ. If we have Christ, we have everything.

Matthew 6:33 *But seek ye first the kingdom of God, and his righteousness; and all these things shall be added unto you (KJV).*

He tells us to seek His kingdom and His righteousness. His kingdom is the domain over which He has sovereign, authority, and rule. But what is His righteousness? Or should I say, who is His righteousness? The apostle Paul tells us in

I Corinthians 1:30, that God made Christ His righteousness. Therefore, Christ is absolutely the righteousness of God, (Philippians 3:9) so that through *His* substitution, *we* could be the righteousness of God (II Corinthians 5:21). This part is an act of our faith. It is a prerequisite to receiving the things. If we don't get this part right, then "all these things…added", is null and void. In other words, you can't fake this. We can't just seek him for the things (John 6:26-27) and expect Him to be pleased, and have His favor on our lives. Even when we do the right things, if we do them for the wrong reasons, we still won't get the results we are looking for from God. As a matter of fact, if we do this, then God isn't getting what He is looking for from us. He sees behind our facades right to our heart's true motive and intent.

We cannot fool God. If you look at St. John 6:26, we see that the people of Christ's day couldn't fool Him either. He exposed their true desire. We must be careful not to bring our greed into how we seek His presence. We must first acknowledge the elephant of greed in the room, and admit our sin, so that it doesn't taint our worship and affect our relationship with Christ. We need to learn that what we really need is Christ and not the things. The things result from a relationship with Him. The relationship is the important part. This is why He came, not to give us stuff, but to give us life everlasting. It is the relationship with Him that ensures that kind of life.

John tells us that He will not cast away those that come to Him, who believe in Him, and seek a relationship with Him (vs 37). This relationship is the foundation on which everything else is built. Once this foundation has been firmly established, then, and only then, are we able to apply passages like Philippians 4:19, "But my God shall supply all your need according to His riches in glory by Christ Jesus", and have it truly mean something. For any of this to work like it's supposed to, in complete balance of relationship and blessing, Christ must be at the core of everything. We cannot place Him first in a few things, and think we can handle the rest on our own. This "Thanks, Lord for your help, but I can take it from here", kind of attitude is not going to fly, at least not straight, anyway. If we want to arrive at the destination God has mapped out for us, with good success and favor, then in all things, Christ must be the first, the last, and the head of every detail of our lives in between.

CHAPTER 8
The Battle Against Stinking Thinking

"For as [a man] thinks in his heart, so is he."

Imagine, if you will, a big city like New York, Chicago, or Los Angeles. Now imagine that you've never been to a big city before, and you've just been dropped off downtown, in the middle of the day. What would you see? How would you feel? What would your overall experience be like? It would probably be busy, and full of hustle and bustle. Perhaps it would seem chaotic. The traffic. The people. The noise. The congestion. The pollution. More than likely, you'd be overwhelmed.

Now imagine those same scenarios, but instead of a big city, you're actually inside of someone's mind. It would probably be just as overwhelming. Thoughts would be like traffic. There would be images of people. The noise of both potential and past conversations would fill your ears. And then there would be the congestion of memories, both current and of long ago. I know I've used this analogy before, but our minds really are like cities. Thoughts are what live in them. There's the inner city, where thoughts are congested and stacked one on top of the other. Away from the center is like the suburbs, where the more pleasant thoughts live. We have our corporate hub, where our thoughts take care of business. There are dark allies, where shady thoughts hang out. And there is the seething underbelly of the mind, where dark and more blatantly evil thoughts plan their deeds. Our minds also have a nightlife. And I'll just leave that up to your imaginations. And we also have entertainment and sports arenas, where thoughts are entertained, or where thoughts entertain us. So, how we live in our heads is how we live outwardly. In other words, our thought life eventually becomes our real life.

Proverbs 23:6-7 tells us... The man in the scripture would

seem on the surface to be kind because he offered food and drink. He was hospitable. But the Bible says he is (stingy), not because of what he says, but because of what he thinks in his heart. This may be hard for some of us to hear but our thoughts define who we really are. It is not our intentions, our polite manners, or how others view us that make us who we are. It is how we think on the inside. Verse 7a says "for as he thinks in his heart, so is he."(KJV). In other words, it's not what a man thinks he is, it's what a man thinks, he is. Therefore, what we think ourselves to be is not what we are. But, what and how we think is what we truly become.

When we have wronged others, we expect to be judged by our intentions alone. "Hey man, I'm sorry. But I didn't mean to do it". But when we have been wronged, we expect others to be judged by their actions alone. "I know you're sorry, but that doesn't matter, you still have to pay for this." This is how we are with God. We are asking Him to judge us on how we intended to be, how we wanted to be, or how we think we would be. But he calls us out based on our thought life because that is who we are inwardly, despite what we show outwardly. There is a saying that states, "Watch your thoughts. Thoughts become words. Watch your words. Words become actions. Watch your actions. Actions become character. Watch your character. Character becomes your destiny."

I think we just stepped into a different scope of warfare here. If our minds are like cities, and our thought life is what lives in them, then we just moved into urban warfare. Any soldier that has fought in the Middle East can attest to the fact that, urban warfare takes a whole different strategic style of fighting. There are buildings and urban obstacles with which to contend. With those obstacles come the dangers of IEDs (improvised explosive devices), and booby traps. The local population that needs to be protected could potentially be working with the enemy. Or the enemy could use some of those locals as human shields during his attacks. This is the same kind of warfare we have inside of our hearts and minds. We must use the same kind of strategy in order to navigate our own thoughts. We must be vigilant about our thoughts at all times because all thoughts aren't necessarily good, even when they seem good on the surface. A "good" thought may be a shield used by our flesh to set us up for attack. The enemy may exploit our own thought processes (mental structures) to set an ambush, using explosive ideas.

So what are the strategies needed to fight in this "urban" warfare of the mind? Unfortunately, there is no way to plan for every scenario of the enemy. There are just too many possibilities and too many directions of attack. However, there are some general, overall training that we can go through, that will cover any situation the enemy could throw our way. In this type of warfare, three things are needed. They are repentance, conversion, and spiritual identity.

Mark 1:14-15 (ESV) says, "Now after John was arrested, Jesus came into Galilee, proclaiming the gospel of God, and saying, 'The time is fulfilled, and the kingdom of God is at hand; repent and believe in the gospel.'" Afterwards, Luke 22:31-32 (KJV) says, "And the Lord said, Simon, Simon, behold, Satan hath desired to have you, that he may sift you as wheat: But I have prayed for thee, that thy faith fail not: and when thou art converted, strengthen thy brethren." Repentance, according to Strong's Concordance of the King James Bible is from:

3340 metanoeo' Greek. Verb. (met-an-o-eh'-o) (from 3326/meta, "changed after being with" and 3539/noieo, "think") - properly, "think differently after," "after a change of mind"; to repent (literally, "think differently afterwards"). I repent, change my mind, change the inner man (particularly with reference to acceptance of the will of God), repent.

The definition of conversion, according to Strong's is from:
1994 epistrepho' Greek. Verb. (ep-ee-stref'-o) (from 1909 and 4762; to revert [lit., fig. or mor.]):- come (go) again, convert, (re-) turn (about, again). I turn (back) to (towards); I come to myself.

Let's talk about repentance first. The definition, simply put, means to change our minds. It is to change from what we previously thought to a new way of thinking. In this case, it's changing from our thinking about life to God's way of thinking. In other words, we have to agree with God. How do we do that? Well, I'm glad you asked. Remember, Paul was in the middle of his struggle when he spoke these words. So, look at how he agreed with God.

Romans 7:12 (ESV) "So the law is holy, and the commandment is holy and righteous and good."

Romans 7:14 (ESV) "For we know that the law is spiritual, but I am of the flesh, sold under sin."

Romans 7:16 (ESV) "Now if I do what I do not want, I agree with the law, that it is good."

Romans 7:18 (ESV) "For I know that nothing good dwells in me, that is, in my flesh. For I have the desire to do what is right, but not the ability to carry it out."

Romans 7:24 (NKJV) "O wretched man that I am! Who will deliver me from this body of death?"

He agrees with God concerning God's word. He agrees with

God concerning himself. And he agrees with God concerning the fact that he needs help. It seems obvious in Romans 7:25, that he agrees with God that God, through Christ is the one to give him that help. We must do the same, and come to the same conclusions Paul did. These are the terms and agreements portion of our faith.

As believers, I think we sometimes "sign on" in this section, without fully understanding all that it entails. Read His word and seek to understand it. It will literally save your life.

The next thing we need is to be converted. If repentance means to change our minds, then conversion, means to walk back toward God. Then, when we get to Him, walk with Him. How, exactly do we do that? Well, I'm glad you asked. Again, Paul finds the answers he was looking for and shares them with us. "Thanks be to God, through Jesus Christ our Lord! So then, I myself serve the law of God with my mind, but with my flesh, I serve the law of sin. There is therefore now no condemnation for those who are in Christ Jesus. For the law of the

Spirit of life has set you free in Christ Jesus from the law of sin and death. For God has done what the law, weakened by the flesh, could not do. By sending his own Son in the likeness of sinful flesh and for sin, he condemned sin in the flesh, in order that the righteous requirement of the law might be fulfilled in us, who walk not according to the flesh but according to the Spirit. For those who live according to the flesh set their minds on the things of the flesh, but those who live according to the Spirit set their minds on the things of the Spirit. For to set the mind on the flesh is death, but to set the mind on the Spirit is life and peace. For the mind that is set on the flesh is hostile to God, for it does not submit to God's law; indeed, it cannot. Those who are in the flesh cannot please God" Romans 7:25 - 8:8 (ESV).

Paul tells us the "how", the "why", and most importantly, "who", it is Christ. Walk toward God. Walk with God. This is the strategy that causes us to have victory. And not just victory for ourselves, but according to Luke 22:32, it will allow us to help others to victory as well.

Finally, we have to have an understanding of our spiritual

identity. This is who we are in God. Or better stated, what God intended us to be when He created us. Many of us don't know who we really are or who we really represent. Even from the time before we are born, the enemy uses the things in this world to redefine who we are and keep us in the dark about our true identities. He uses our social and economic status, our parents and close relatives, childhood friends, teachers, and co-workers, etc. Most, if not all of these people, never once stop to ask God who we really are. They simply thrust their own desires and expectations upon us. And by the time we are well into adulthood, many of us are still trying to figure out who we are. We walk around with a false sense of self. We then try to cram that into God's will for our lives, then wonder why our plans don't work.

There is an internal struggle against the forces of darkness to keep us ignorant of our real selves. Many of us may not realize that this is also what our warfare is all about. The enemy is trying to keep us ignorant. An ignorant people is a conquered people. So how do we regain the ground of our identity after we have lost so much of it up to this point? Well, I'm glad you asked. Again, Paul is really nailing it here for us. II Corinthians 10:3-5 "For though we walk (live) in the flesh, we are not carrying on our warfare according to the flesh and using mere human weapons. For the weapons of our warfare are not physical [weapons of flesh and blood], but they are mighty before God for the overthrow and destruction of strongholds, [In as much as we] refute arguments and theories and reasonings and every proud and lofty thing that sets itself up against the [true] knowledge of God; and we lead every thought and purpose away captive into the obedience of Christ (the Messiah, the Anointed One)" (AMPC).

During Desert Storm, there was a lot of focus in the news media about the types of weapons being used by both sides. One, in particular, was the enemy's scud missile. These were a series of tactical ballistic missiles developed by the Soviet Union. They were widely exported to second and third world countries, Iraq being one of them. The coalition forces' answer to this missile was SAMs (Surface to Air Missiles). These were extremely effective in shooting down the majority of the scuds. As believers, we need to use our own version of SAMs in a spiritual way. I refer to it as our Spiritually Armed Mindset (S.A.M.s). SAMs are our minds armed with the knowledge of God's Word concerning our identities in

Christ. They are passages like, II Corinthians 5:21 (ESV) "For He made Him who knew no sin to be sin for us, that we might become the righteousness of God in Him". I John 4:17 "Love has been perfected among us in this: that we may have boldness in the day of judgment; because as He is, so are we in this world" (KJV). Reading and understanding His Word not only will save your life, but it will give you a better quality of life, by destroying the very weapons the enemy uses against us. Isaiah 54:17 (NKJV) "No weapon formed against you shall prosper, and every tongue which rises against you in judgment you shall condemn. This is the heritage of the servants of the Lord, and their righteousness is from Me," Says the Lord". That quality of life is our heritage and our righteousness, which is from Christ Himself.

CHAPTER 9
Whispering Behind Enemy Lines

The Importance of Having a Clear and Consistent Prayer Life

I have never been in combat. I have never served in any branch of the military. Sometimes though, I wish I had. I feel as though military life would have taught me some things, a lot sooner. But in the words of Job, "[God] knows the way that I take". However, I have a great respect for those who have served. And I have an even greater respect for those who have served through combat. My father is one of those individuals. He is a veteran of the Vietnam War, and served in the Air Force from 1963 - 1968. Growing up, I remember my dad loved watching war movies, especially ones from the Vietnam era. Every time there was an F-4 fighter jet in the picture, he'd almost raise up out of his seat. He would yell,

"That's my baby right there!" You see, he was assigned to one of the ground support units for the F-4 Phantom 2 fighter jets. This aircraft was the main fighter jet for the United States Air Force, the Navy and the Marines during Vietnam. When I got old enough to understand what the movies were about, I would often ask him about the accuracy of particular movies. He would say, "Son, it was pretty much just like that".

I remember watching one movie where there was a soldier in charge of communications. He had on a backpack with a portable radio unit in it. His platoon was taking on heavy fire and was pinned down in their position. The officer was giving their coordinates and asking to be evacuated. For a long time there was no answer. After calling several times, there finally was a voice on the other end, saying there was a chopper on the way to their position. Another movie I watched had a platoon with orders to only patrol and report while in the field. While on maneuvers, they spotted the enemy, but the enemy didn't see them. The communications officer whispered on the radio, asking for further instructions, wanting to know whether to engage the enemy. The instructions came back over the radio, "Do not engage the enemy. Do not fire unless fired upon. I repeat. Do not fire unless fired upon." The platoon ended up being discovered by the enemy, and some idiot got a little jumpy, and fired first. This opened up barrage of gunfire that quickly turned tragic for most of the platoon.

The guy with the backpack radio was always intriguing to me. Because of his gear, he always stood out. Besides the platoon leader, he seemed to have the next most important job. His job was to send and receive messages vital for the platoon's survival in the field. He was also responsible for knowing the platoon's position and coordinates at all times. The messages both given and received, were more than just communication. They were part of the warfare itself, because they determined how the platoon fought its battles. "And take the helmet of salvation, and the sword of the Spirit, which is the word of God; praying always with all prayer and supplication in the Spirit, being watchful to this end with all perseverance and supplication for all the saints— and for me, that utterance may be given to me, that I may open my mouth boldly to make known the mystery of the gospel, for which I am an ambassador in chains; that in it I may speak boldly, as I ought to speak" (Ephesians 6:17-20 NKJV).

This portion of Paul's letter to the Ephesians shows that prayer is more than just communication during warfare. Prayer is warfare in itself. "...Take...the sword of the Spirit...the word of God; praying..." Prayer is warfare because prayer is actually how we wield the sword of the Spirit. This is how we battle. Prayer is absolutely essential for victory in day-to-day living. If we do not pray, then we are missing a key component to our fight. It is like having a magnificent sword, but never picking it up during battle. It becomes useless to us. And not picking up that sword becomes a fatal mistake. This is probably why many believers are not very adept with the word of God, because the word of God requires prayer in order to swing it, and many believers struggle with prayer. Satan uses our flesh to undermine our prayer life, so that we do not use a major weapon in our arsenal that not only can defeat him, but has the ability to neutralize his attacks against us as well.

The correlation between that soldier with the radio backpack and us, when it comes to prayer, is mind blowing. Just like that soldier, we have the ability to communicate our position, call in "air strikes" and "air support", ask for reinforcements, ask for transport or rescue out of the area, and receive info about advancements and retreats. And you can find all of that right in the Bible. Communication of position is found in Exodus 2:23-25 (Israel cries to God in Egypt). Air strikes are found in I Kings 18:24, 36-38 (Elijah calls down fire from heaven). Air support can be found in Daniel 10:12-13, 20-21 (An angel answers Daniel after 21 days). We can ask for reinforcements according to II Kings 6:16-18 (Chariots of fire surround the Assyrian army on Elisha's behalf). If rescue is needed, we can refer to Psalms 34:6-7 (King David cried to

God in his distress). If we need to advance in warfare, look to I Chronicles 14:14-15 (King David inquires of God against the Philistines), or I Samuel 30:8 (King David inquires of God at Ziklag). If we need to know whether to stand our ground or retreat then try II Chronicles 18:14a, and 16 (King Ahab inquires of God through the prophet Micaiah). This is the totality of warfare. And it is all done through prayer. There is a meme I've seen on the Internet, with a picture of a knight in armor, on one knee, with his head down. The caption reads, "The devil thought he caught me with my head hung down, until I lifted my head and said, 'Amen'." I always pictured Satan as having the most horrified look on his face, after the realization that the person he was attacking was a person of prayer. The most frightening thing to the kingdom of darkness is a believer who prays.

Prayer answers all of the questions. It answers who, what, where, when, and how. WHO do we pray to? God (II Chronicles 33:18; Nehemiah 4:9; Psalms 42:8, 69:13; Daniel 9:3; Acts 12:5; Philippians 4:6). WHAT do we pray about?

Everything (Philippians 4:6). WHERE do we pray? Everywhere (I Timothy 2:8). WHEN do we pray? Always (Luke 18:1, 21:36; I Thessalonians 5:17; II Thessalonians 1:11). HOW do we pray? With all prayer and supplication (Ephesians 6:18). Prayer is more than just words we say, to some guy we can't see, who is out there somewhere. We cannot pray without involving or engaging our hearts in the process. The same way we receive salvation, belief and confession, is the same way our prayers are answered. Don't just pray. To whom are you praying? Don't believe in prayer. Believe in the one to whom you pray. We pray to show that we have faith. But we cannot simply have faith in faith itself. On whom is the foundation of our faith based? It should be the foundation of Christ. We cannot receive answered prayers without faith in Christ (James 1:6-7). And we cannot please God without faith in Christ either (Hebrews 11:6).

We've been discussing prayer as warfare. Why prayer? The reason is because prayer is an unconventional fighting technique for an unconventional war. Conventional warfare uses guns, bombs, aircraft, missiles, tanks, targeting systems, etc. In prayer, the weapon of choice is a sword, i.e. the Word of God. Spiritual swordplay combines the Word of God with spiritual, hand-to-hand combat techniques (II Samuel 22:35; Psalms 144:1). We are made in the image and likeness of God (Genesis 1:26). Therefore, we have the ability to use the Word as God does (Isaiah 49:2a, Revelation 1:16; 2:16; 19:15; 19:21). Everything listed in Revelations chapters 1, 2, and 19 is referring to Christ. Also, Isaiah 49:2, states that He will make our mouth like a sharp sword. We see Christ use the Word in hand-to-hand combat fashion when He encounters Satan, after his time in the wilderness (Matthew 4:1-11). His fighting style is made apparent with the statement, "It is written", against which, there is no defense.

In our warfare of prayer, Paul admonishes us, in Ephesians 6:18, to pray with all prayer. In my studies, I have found that all prayer encompasses at least five areas. They are petition, intercession, thanksgiving, praise, and repentance. Petition is prayer to God, on behalf of ourselves. "Father bless me with a new job", "Lord help me control my temper", or "God help me make the right decision" are some examples (Luke 11:3-4; 11:9-10; James 1:5-6). We need to remember, when petitioning God, especially in the area of deliverance from the flesh, it is impossible to ask for help from Him and not receive it (Luke 11:11-13; James 1:5). Intercession is prayer to God on behalf of others. "Lord, bless my friend" or "Lord, heal my co-worker" are examples of intercession (Isaiah 53:12; Romans 8:26-27; Acts 12:5; Ephesians 6:18-19).Thanksgiving is prayer of gratitude to God. Examples of this are "Father, thank you for blessing my friend", and "Thank you Lord for healing my co-worker". (Nehemiah 11:17 [priestly assignment]; Psalms 26:7; 100:4; Colossians 4:2; Philippians 4:6). Repentance is prayer to God for forgiveness of sins (Psalms 51:1-2; 51:9-12; Luke 15:18-19; 18:13-14). A prayer of praise is a prayer of compliment to God about His character. An example of this would be, "God you are wonderful, mighty, awesome, magnificent..." etc.

(Psalms 34:1-3; 145:3; Daniel 4:34-37; Acts 16:25).

As we can see, praying with all prayer is like the MMA (mixed martial arts) of spiritual warfare. This is incredible warfare. We can war on behalf of ourselves, and others. We can be tenacious in repentance, persistent in our gratitude, and relentless in our praise of the Most High. All of this will keep our flesh in check and Satan running for the nearest hole in the ground. But be on guard for pride. Even when it comes to prayer we can get prideful. The success of our prayers can make us do one of two things. It can cause our prayers to be devoid of faith, by making us think that it is "our" prayer rather than God's power at work. Or, it can cause us to forget our need and dependency on God, and we stop praying. To believe in only our prayers or to not pray at all, are both arrogant. The moment we find ourselves saying, "I got this", then we are pretty much done. It is only a matter of time before we stumble and fall. We must keep our prayer life going strong and consistent. We must also keep our faith in God's power at the center of our prayers, so that our prayers are answered, our enemies are defeated, and we show forth the victory that is in Christ to others.

CHAPTER 10
Spiritual Blackmail

Secrecy, Exposure, and Accountability

There is a story I heard some time ago about two brothers that lived on their father's farm. Their father had all kinds of animals on the farm. His favorites, however, were a pair of prize-winning ducks that had won first place at the county fair. One day the brothers took their BB guns and went out to do some target practice. The older brother was almost always the better shot. "I bet you can't hit that over there". "I bet you I can." This was their conversation for quite a while. The younger brother, wanting to prove himself to his older brother, suggested that he take aim at one of the prized ducks. The older brother, doubting his younger brother's aim, dared him to do so. His aim ended up being true to its mark. However, he inadvertently killed his father's prize-winning duck. The younger brother was terrified at the prospect of his father finding out what he had done. The older brother came to his rescue by offering to cover it up, in exchange for his brother doing his chores for that day. His brother gladly agreed, and the deed was done. The next day, after supper, the older brother asked the younger to do his dishes for him. He said "No", but his brother replied, "Duck, duck, duck". The younger brother relented and did the dishes. The next day the older brother asked him to do his barnyard chores. The younger brother said, "No". The older brother replied, "Duck, duck, duck". His younger brother grudgingly gave in and did the chores. This went on for a few days, but the younger brother, not willing to keep up the charade, went to his father and confessed. The father had already found the duck buried in a shallow grave just a few days earlier. He shared how pleased he was that his son came forward on his own volition, and promptly forgave his youngest son. Later that day the older brother asked the younger brother to chop wood for him so that he could go and hang out with his friends. His brother confidently replied, "No way". The older brother said, "Duck, duck, duck". The younger brother replied, "You can say duck all you want, but I've already talked to dad about it, and you can't make me do your chores anymore. Besides, dad found the duck you buried. He wants to talk to you".

When it comes to our sins, we're like both brothers. We're either like the older brother, trying to be slick, and use the secrecy of our sin as a means to get what we want. Or, we are like the younger, so afraid of being found out, that we lock ourselves into a single, devastating course of action. Either way, unbeknownst to us, the Father already knows, and is just waiting for us to come to him so He can promptly forgive us.

The strength of blackmail is secrecy. As long as the deed remained secret, his brother's blackmail remained intact. The strength of secrecy is fear (I John 4:18). As long as the younger brother was afraid of his father finding out what he had done, the older brother had the upper hand. He could force his younger brother to do almost anything. Love is what breaks the back of fear (I John 4:18). When the father told his youngest son that he already knew about the duck, and immediately forgave him anyway, the father showed his love. His son was no longer afraid (I John 4:17). Exposure breaks the power of secrecy (Proverbs 27:5). The moment the younger brother confessed to his father (the one from whom the secret was being kept), it was no longer a secret. His son was now relieved. The cushion of exposure is love (I Peter 4:8). For the younger son, the fact that the father responded in love softened the blow of the secret being exposed. It wasn't as bad as he thought.

This is the detrimental effect of fear in our lives. We often imagine things far worse than they end up being. A long time ago I heard of one definition of fear as an acronym. F.E.A.R. is false evidence appearing real. Just like with the younger brother, the evidence, however false, appears so real, that there seems to be no alternate course of action. Exposure is what we are afraid of. It is not a fear of merely being uncovered, but a fear of what that uncovering might entail. It is a fear that is perceived, and not one that is based on any real or concrete evidence. The perceived fear is twofold. First it is the fear of judgment of others, or the loss of the appearance of righteousness in the eyes of others. This is one of the world's biggest statements. "Hey! Don't judge me". We don't want people pointing fingers at us, talking down about our character, or gossiping about us behind our backs. And even when the accusations are true, we still don't want to appear less righteous to others than we previously did. The second thing we fear is a loss of respect from others. We don't want to seem as though we are less, in the eyes of others, than we once were. We fear being knocked down a few rungs on the ladder of life. After it's all said and done, we still want to be held in high regard.

We just talked about the fear of perceived loss due to exposure, but there are some real and actual losses associated with exposure. These losses are familiarity, privacy, and control. Loss of familiarity is one that takes a long time to come to grips with. We keep trying alternatives that we're used to or comfortable with to deal with our sin issue. This is tantamount to insanity. You know, it's doing the same thing over and over again and expecting a different result. We want freedom from sin on our terms. And like our familiar efforts, it doesn't work. We know that God's way works. And we want to do God's will. However, we know that God's way requires exposure. The truth is we are more interested in the judgment and perception of others than we are in truly getting free. It takes many of us some time before we get fed up enough with sin to the point that we don't care what others think. We just want to be free.

As far as exposure is concerned, the loss of privacy is a very real loss to come to terms with. The secret is out. The cat is out of the bag (And why would anyone put a cat in a bag anyway? It's not like God doesn't know it's there). Our problem with the loss of privacy is not with God, but with our fellow human beings. I just don't want YOU to know, even if you mean well (Galatians 6:1). Not only does God know, but often times, people know about our sin too. Our attempt to hide our sin is, at best futile, and at worst, downright pathetic. Sometimes we're the last to know that everybody knows. At this point, we often feel naked and vulnerable. We fear that we'll be taken advantage of in our vulnerability. We are often skeptical of the love and spirituality of those around us. Our brothers' and sisters' good intentions are made known when they bring restoration and our sin is known to them, but not revealed to others (Proverbs 12:16; 17:19; Galatians 6:1; I Peter 4:8).

Finally, there is the loss of control. The loss of control is really the loss of an illusion. It is an illusion because we never really had control in the first place. What was actually in control was our flesh. And because our flesh was in control that meant that sin was in control as well (Romans 7:16-17, 23, 25). Finding out that our control was just an illusion can be a scary prospect, but it can also be a rewarding one, if we call out to our Heavenly Father to pull us to freedom.

And speaking of loss, exposure, even when it is working for our good, brings a certain amount of loss. No matter how great or small, loss brings a certain amount of grief. Grief, as we all know, has to be dealt with in stages. When it comes time for exposure, our prayers are often centered around, or filtered through the stages of grief. While some of us may be familiar with five stages of grief, some psychologists now recognize seven stages to this process. The five original stages of grief are denial, anger, bargaining, depression, and acceptance. For the purposes that we will talk about, I will refer to the seven stages of grief. They are as follows:

1.) Shock & Denial - The reaction of numbed disbelief after learning of the loss. Often accompanied by the refusal to believe in the reality of the loss.

2.) Pain & Guilt - Suffering and emotional distress often experienced after the shock wears off. Feelings of remorse or regret over things done or not done prior to the loss.

3.) Anger - Feelings of annoyance, displeasure, and hostility over the loss.

4.) Bargaining - The negotiation of terms and conditions of the loss with "the powers that be", despite the reality of the loss already occurring.

5.) Depression, reflection, loneliness - A period of sadness or sorrow due to the loss. Sorrowful thought or consideration of what has been lost. The feeling of isolation (real or imagined) that occurs due to the realization of the magnitude of the loss.

6.) Reconstruction - The working through of realistic, practical, and constructive solutions to problems posed by life after the loss.

7.) Acceptance & hope - The willingness to tolerate or cope with the reality of the unpleasant or difficult situation brought on by the loss. The actual planning and looking forward to the future without pain, suffering, or distress despite the prior loss.

These stages are loosely interpreted, and have plenty of individual variation. They also do not necessarily follow in chronological order, and may sometimes overlap one another from time to time.

Our prayers are often filtered through these stages of grief. We pray that we can solve our problems without having to be exposed at all. We repent of our sin (at least for the moment), and ask God to help us with our emotional distresses. We get mad at ourselves for being disobedient to God in the first place. We negotiate and make grandiose promises to God in exchange for Him making it all go away. And we reflect on how good things were before we fell into sin. But hopefully, we recognize the need for obedience, and work with the Holy Spirit as He does His work within our hearts. And also learn to accept the reality of our consequences, and look forward to a lifestyle of obedience to God's word. The things we gain through Godly exposure far outweigh the losses we will ever endure from them.

If you have ever had an open wound, you know that it cannot remain exposed, but must be covered, in order for it to heal properly. While exposure destroys the power of secrecy, it is not enough by itself, to bring us back to full restoration. Accountability is necessary because, promises made in secret are rarely kept without someone to ensure that we actually follow through with them. We need accountability to cover us while we heal from the inside. Accountability is the bandage that protects us from the infections of the world. We have to participate in the restoration process and allow spiritual people to cover us, so that healing can take place (Galatians 6:1-2). If we thought exposure made us loose a little privacy, then accountability is the loss of privacy to the tenth power. Within accountability, there is continual exposure or transparency to the one to whom we are accountable. In this instance, transparency is the private exposure to only an individual who has the capacity to watch for our souls. We open ourselves to this individual's wise and spiritual assessment of our recovery process, without fear of abuse or personal judgment.

Because accountability can sometimes be demanding, we can often develop resentment to the routine assessment and the loss of privacy. If we find ourselves in this dilemma, then there is a good chance pride has crept in. Pride resents accountability. Pride will cause us to seek independence before our healing is complete. This threatens to derail our progress, and drive us back into secrecy and bondage. Pride threatened to stop my own process of recovery while dealing with pornography. Because I had been in "church" for so long, I felt as though I should have been further along in my healing precession than I was. I was considering longevity in the faith as a reason not to need or ask for help. This was an expectation that was not based in reality. The reality was that I had unresolved issues of the soul that had yet to be worked through, regardless of how long I had been in the faith. Accountability holds our feet to the fire, allowing the Holy Spirit to do His work of uprooting the issues of our souls.

Remember, pride is one of those three areas of sin we all are tempted in; the pride of life, the lust of the flesh, and the lust of the eye. In the Garden of Eden, Eve saw that the fruit was good for food. Many of us feed off of the sympathy and pity of others as we struggle with our issues of sin. After all, what are we without our sob story? We hold on to it like it is a badge of honor because of our suffering.

Eve also saw that the fruit was pleasing to the eye. Sometimes it is more important for us to be pleased by how we are viewed by others, even if that view is based off of a lie. We are fooled into thinking that because others are pleased with how we appear, that God is the same way. We end up striving for God's approval from a "works" based salvation that can never be attained. So we end up faking it. And if we are not careful, we can fake it for so long that we no longer are able to recognize the truth. We develop a delusion of the soul, and start believing the very lie we used to cover up our sin (II Thessalonians 2:11-12).

The enemy fights us with weapons like secrecy to strengthen his spiritual blackmail over us. He uses the torment of fear to strengthen the secret. However, Godly exposure nullifies the power of secrecy. And the perfection of God's love both cushions the landing from exposure, and altogether annihilates all fear. The greatest weapon our Heavenly Father ever gave us was His love. But, He didn't just give us some emotional feeling or an abstract force. He gave us his perfection. He gave us love, in the person of Jesus Christ.

For God so loved the world that He gave His only begotten Son, that whoever believes in Him should not perish but have everlasting life. For God did not send His Son into the world to condemn the world, but that the world through Him might be saved (John 3:16-17 NKJV).

LARRY SHELBY, JR.

ABOUT THE AUTHOR

Apostle (Designee) Larry Shelby Jr. is a senior leader at His Glory International Covenant Ministries in Chicago, Illinois, where he serves as Resident Covenant Church Planter. He is the founder and senior pastor of Stones of Fire Kingdom Ministries in Gary, Indiana. He also serves as Regional Director for the central division of His Glory International Covenant Network, the national and international extension of HGICM. He has been a servant of the gospel for over 26 years. He has been married to his lovely wife Sherell for 25 years, and they have three children, Imani, Domonique, and Lauren.

www.ingramcontent.com/pod-product-compliance
Lightning Source LLC
Chambersburg PA
CBHW070453090426
42735CB00012B/2532